THE 7 NO NOS

A GUIDE TO
AWAKENING & FREEDOM

KAY CORDELL WHITAKER

The Author of *The Reluctant Shaman,*
Sacred Link and *The Weavings*

A WORLD IN BALANCE
WWW.KATASEE.COM
WWW.LINKTR.EE/KATASEE

PRAISE FOR THE 7 NO NOS

"*The 7 No Nos* is an elegant, accessible, and fun book that speaks directly to the heart. Its principles serve as clear guideposts for moving out of the "yuck" and into the "yum"! The teachings and practices are simple, enjoyable, and incredibly powerful. It is a refreshing reminder to follow what we intuitively know to be true and to love unconditionally."

- DeAnna R. Pickett, MS, LPC

"Kay has masterfully taken ancient teachings thousands of years old and transformed them into a fresh, accessible book and set of practices perfectly suited for our modern world. *The 7 No Nos* are truly for everyone—no exceptions.

It's thrilling to have a book like this out there. I can already envision a future where we teach these simple, profound principles to our children alongside their ABCs.

The practices themselves are not only enjoyable—they're transformative. The moment you start doing them, you can actually feel a shift begin.

Immense gratitude to Kay for sharing these timeless teachings and powerful practices with us all."

- Lora Keddie, Ka Ta See Shaman

"*The 7 No No's* is the Four Agreements of the Ka Ta See. Full of life changing wisdom in easily digestible form, Kay lays out simple concrete actions anyone can take to break free from the unhealthy programming so prevalent in the modern world and rediscover how to joyfully live their Song - aka your life purpose.

This book is a true gift to anyone seeking a life of deeper meaning no matter the length of time they've spent on the journey. Whether these truths come as a revelation or a reminder, they all come as friends. This is one of those books I will be buying regularly and spreading around.

Thank you Kay for taking such deep wisdom and bringing it to life in a poetic approachable manner. The world needs this!"

- Charity Gaye Finnestad, author *Hollywood in Heels*

Published by A World In Balance
7 Avenida Vista Grande B7-323
Santa Fe, NM 87508-9198
song@katasee.com
www.katasee.com
www.linktr.ee/katasee
505-466-3387

Petroglyph Illustrations: Kay Cordell Whitaker

Genre: Spiritual, Self-Help

FIRST EDITION

DEDICATION

This book is dedicated in respect and gratitude to our Mother, our planet Earth, for all that she has continually given to us, with a prayer for her rapid and gentle healing, that we may earn the opportunity to move into the future with her in a good way.

CONTENTS

AUTHOR'S NOTES

AN INVITATION TO YOUR OWN SONG

For millennia, ancient wisdom has been safeguarded in hidden corners of the world—whispered in small circles, preserved by keepers of sacred traditions, and shielded from a world not yet ready to hear it.

These teachings, held in secret by cultures like the Peruvian Ka Ta See and the pre-flood Egyptian mysteries, were oral treasures, passed down with reverence and protected by the weight of silence.

Now, in our time, the Ka Ta See lineage carriers—my teachers, Domano and Chea Hetaka of Peru, and a Berber wisdom keeper from Egypt—have declared it the hour to share these gifts with humanity. The world is ready, and so are you.

By a stroke of extraordinary fortune, I was entrusted with these teachings from two distant traditions, one rooted in the Andes and the lost land of Lemuria, the other in the sands of Egypt and the echoes of Atlantis.

Over the years of study, I discovered a profound unity: their philosophies and intricate healing practices were nearly identical, revealing a universal truth about who we are and how we can live.

These ancient ways, once guarded under threat of death, are not about intellectual debate or arcane details. They are about "feeling"—your emotions, your senses, your innate intuition. They speak to the heart of what it means to be human, to be whole, to be a "Song."

In the language of the Hetakas, your Song is the vibrant, eternal essence of your being—a unique melody of spirit, emotions, and body, woven into the cosmic symphony of all existence—it is who and what you are.

Yet, our modern world, with its rush and noise, has taught us to forget this melody. We've inherited a sickness of disconnection—dimmed attention, dulled feelings, and a longing for something more. The ancients warn that without awakening from this disharmony, we risk losing ourselves.

But they also offer hope: by unlearning these patterns, we can lift the blinders, see the world's breathtaking beauty, and build a future grounded in love, truth, and creativity.

This book is your calling to that awakening. The 7 No Nos are not rules but gentle nudges—practical tools to question the lies, release the burdens, and rediscover the deep joy of your Song. They are a bridge between ancient wisdom and modern life, accessible to all, whether you're a spiritual seeker or simply curious about a better way to live.

I urge you not to overthink these pages. Let the words sink into your heart. Read slowly, perhaps a page or two at a time, and pause to feel their resonance. Engage the practices with your senses, your emotions, your whole being. As the ancients teach, feeling is the key—where the magic of transformation unfolds.

My journey with these teachings has been one of wonder, challenge, and profound joy. Through the Hetakas' warmth and the Egyptian keeper's quiet strength, I learned that we are not alone in our longing for connection.

Across the globe, indigenous wisdom keepers are sharing their sacred knowledge, urging us to weave a new world together. This is the realm of Song—a world where we overcome our collective sickness, where love, beauty, and self-sovereignty flourish.

Join me in this great adventure. Let your Song sing, and let's create a symphony of awakening, together.

With love and gratitude,

Kay Cordell Whitaker

Ka Ta See Lineage Keeper,
Storyteller Shaman of the Kala Keh Nah Seh Tradition,
Keeper of the Teachings of Isis

THE HEAVENS ARE POURING DOWN TSUNAMIS OF LOVE

In a world swirling with chaos—wild politics, unstable economies, scandals of corruption, and a yearning for something more profound—many of us feel a call from the heart to step away from the chaos for good.

We sense that beneath the troubling noise and loneliness, lies a truth waiting to be uncovered, a love to embrace us, and a beauty to flood our hearts and senses. "The heavens are pouring down tsunamis of love," say the ancients. And we feel it.

We are not the masks we've worn. We are not the fears we've carried. We are a "Song"—vibrant, eternal, deeply connected to, and a part of, "All That Is"—we are a sacred conscious entity in times of crucial growth and change.

This book is your companion on that journey, a guide to remembering the feeling of who and what you are, to step away from the powerless nightmare, to reclaim your unconditional love, your spirit gifts, and your place in this new era of awakening.

The wisdom in these pages draws from ancient traditions—the pre-flood Peruvian Ka Ta See through the voices of Domano and Chea Hetaka, and the pre-flood Egyptian Temple Mysteries. The Hetakas were my teachers for about 13 years before they returned to Peru. In that time they gifted me, among many teachings, seven principles we affectionately call the "No Nos."

The No Nos are a set of invitations to question everything, release what imprisons you, and rediscover your *"Song:"* *the unique and sacred "Totality of your Being."*

These are not rigid rules but gentle nudges toward love, beauty, true freedom and the clarity of the "Field," the "Field of many names."

The ancient teachings that are gifted to you in this book offer practical tools for setting you free, in the modern world and the spiritual world. Each "No

No" is a stepping stone to free yourself from the corruption within—the lies, fears, and habits that mirror the brokenness and corruption we see in the world.

As you transform inwardly, you contribute to a collective awakening, weaving a new world of harmony and connectedness that belongs to all of humanity. Whether you're new to this path or a seasoned seeker, these pages will meet you where you are, offering stories, practices, and insights to guide you home to your Song.

As you read on, listen with the intent to remember. Feel the words as they stir your heart. The path may challenge you, but it will also lead you to freedom.

Let's begin.

PART ONE

THE SECRET HEARTBEAT OF THE NO NOS

SONG   ATTENTION   LOVE

CHAPTER 1

THE BEAUTY OF THE EVER DANCING UNIVERSE

The Universe Is Pouring Itself Onto Our Table

....a banquet for the gods, a tsunami of beauty that sweeps through the cosmos. This beauty is the passion and peace of it all, the splendor of every animal, plant, rock, and human, woven into the Web of Life by Neith, the Egyptian goddess who weaves the world using love as her threads.

As you awaken, you delight more and more in this banquet, inviting its secrets, feeling its beauty and passion in your bones—a haunting, mind-blowing force that drives us to weave a future of love, freedom and creativity into our Field of Aliveness.

Imagine for a moment that you are a melody—a living, breathing Song woven into the vast symphony of the universe. Not a tune you hum absentmindedly, but a profound vibration, a unique harmony of light, love, and consciousness that has echoed its mysteries and beauty through eternity.

This is who you truly are.

The Dream of Forgetting

We come into this world as pure beings, radiant with the knowing of our own Song. As infants, we feel it—the blissful hum of our essence, the curiosity that dances in our eyes, the love that pours from our hearts.

Yet, somewhere along the way, amidst the noise of daily life, we forgot our melody. The world handed us a script, a mask, a false identity, and we began to sing someone else's tune. This book is an invitation to listen to and feel the melodies of our own Song, and to remember the truth that has always been within each of us.

It is an invitation to *question everything!*

The world we are born into has forgotten its melody. It is a world of masks, a bad dream woven from lies, rules, fears, isolation, propaganda, and suspicion. It becomes a self-imposed cage with its door wide open.

From our earliest days, we are taught to conform—to think a certain way, to act a certain way, to be what others demand us to be. Our parents, our teachers, our culture—they hand us a costume and say, "This is you." And because we are young and trusting, we put it on.

The Hetakas—my adopted grandparents and teachers, were wisdom keepers of ancient knowledge from Peru. They called this the "upside-down-backwards-turning-wheel" culture—a monstrous beast that spins us away from our true selves. We learn to value words over feelings, achievements over living presence, fear over love.

Our culture has lost "beauty."

We forget the vastness of who we are, the ancientness of our being, the connectedness we share with all of creation.

The pain of this forgetting is deep—an ache in our soul, a longing we can't quite name. It's the pain of abandoning our Song, of living a life that isn't ours.

What Is Song?

Beneath the layers of conditioning lies your Song—a name gifted to us by the Hetakas, a poetic reference from their native tongue. To them, a Song is not just music; it is sacred, it is the "Totality of your Being." It is your spirit, your emotions, your mind, your physical body—all the unique vibrations, harmonics, and feelings that make you, *you*.

Imagine hearing a piece of music with countless instruments, each note distinct yet blending into a single, extraordinary symphony. That's your Song—a unique individual piece of the Creator, a piece of cosmic beauty, alive with consciousness and a drive to love, to experience and create.

Your Song is ancient, stretching back through countless eons, born from the heart of what we have called "The Creator," "The Great Mystery," or simply "All That Is."

In the Pre-flood Egyptian tradition, this creator is Auset Khemt, called in English, Black Isis—a feminine force of love and diversity who birthed the universe from the deep black unknown. First-born was Mut, an endless outpouring of unconditional love that filled the expanses. Second born was Neith, who wove the unconditional love making our universe. You are a thread in her tapestry of love, a creative spark connected to every other spark across the cosmos....

Feel that for a moment....

You are not alone, not separate, but intimately woven into the fabric of all existence, sharing love, energy and information in an endless dance with "All That Is."

The Sacred Garden of Experience

Why are we here, on this Earth, in these bodies?

Because the universe—Auset Khemt, the Egyptian creation goddess kept secret by the temples—loves beauty, diversity, experience and creating. And the Hetakas teach that true understanding comes only through experiencing life, not just thinking about it.

Earth is no prison; it is a garden, a laboratory of extraordinary possibilities. *We choose* to come here, to take on physical form, to taste the richness of this world through our senses, emotions, and consciousness.

Your physical body is sacred, a treasured, yet temporary aspect of your Song. Through it, you feel the warmth of the sun, the sting of loss, the joy of laughter. It's how you learn about love—what it is and what it isn't.

It's how you explore the depths of emotion, the power of beliefs, the mysteries of the non-material and the material woven together.

It's how we feel and come to know the breathtaking potential of our own humanity.

Our bodies are how we connect to and collect information from the Great Field—our bodies, our DNA, are antennas to *all information*.

Our star people relatives have repeatedly said we humans don't know who we are as a race or individually; that we don't know we carry rare and precious potentials inside us—and it makes them sad.

So what does it mean to be fully human?

Every Song on this planet, every tree, every creature, every human—adds to this multi-sensual garden's beauty—spiritually, emotionally, mentally and physically. We are here to experience it all—physically *and energetically*, to grow, to add our piece to this creation—and to remember.

The Call to Remember

But we forget. As the world wraps us in its demands, we shove our Song into the shadows. We trade our knowingness for masks, our feelings for the emptiness of words, our vastness for a tiny box of "shoulds" and "musts."

The Hetakas say this is the most painful thing we can do—to deny the feeling of who we are, to abandon our own Song.

Even today, we see the denial all around us. We hear artists and intellectuals claiming that we shouldn't make happiness "the goal" of our lives; that it is a fleeting "high" that only brings a big let-down, depression and sadness.

That's because they expect, and even demand, that happiness is only provided from "outside themselves."

They've never known what they think is "happiness" to come to them in any other way. The word "happiness," like most words and their usage in modern languages, is empty, flat and drained of spiritual understanding and feeling. Our actual languages have perpetuated this abandonment for a very, very long time.

Yet, even in our forgetting, the call to awaken persists. It's a whisper in the silence, a pull in the heart, a memory that refuses to fade.

The ancient teachings show you—they demonstrate it to you—that real happiness is the constant state of feeling your Song, feeling who you really are.

They teach that happiness is not a fleeting rush from an outside stimulus. It's the constant state of well-being and joy of your Song; it's the feeling of loving connectedness that can't be severed to everything the cosmos offers. Happiness is the Song's beauty, stability, love, peace and more.

There is something about us that is worth preserving, something so precious and divine.

Your Song has a signature—a beautiful, unique, descriptive feeling that radiates from your being, like light from a bulb. It's the essence of your Totality—carrying your history, your love, your individuality, your connectedness, your happiness. When you were born, you knew this feeling. You lived it, loved it, breathed it, shone it out with every giggle and gaze.

Now, it's time to reclaim it.

Feeling Your Song

Reconnecting with your Song isn't about thinking harder or collecting spiritual tricks. It's about *feeling*—returning to the heart, to the sensations that pulse beneath the chatter of the mind.

The Hetakas teach a practice called the "Ceremony of Finding Your Song," a way to turn your attention inward, to that *"forbidden place where your truth awaits."*

Here, in the stillness, you can feel your ancientness, your vastness, the unconditional love that flows through you.

It's blissful, breathtaking—a taste of the divine that you are.

This feeling isn't meant to stay in ceremony alone—it's a knowingness—it's "beingness." When you put your attention to it, you can carry this feeling into your everyday life.

Imagine moving through your day—working, laughing, resting—while holding the calm, steady awareness of your own truth, your Song.

This is the goal: to live from your real essence, to let it be the foundation of all you do, to identify with it, even amidst the scattered rushing and insanity of the world—you always know this feeling is who and what you really are.

THE PATH OF
THE 7 NO NOS

Awakening is an adventure, a journey of unlearning—of peeling away the masks and thoughtforms that have been drowning out your Song. The "7 No Nos," the wisdom from the Hetakas, are your guides on this path for the rest of your life.

They are not commandments, but invitations to question everything, to feel deeper than you ever thought possible—they are all invitations to free yourself.

Let's explore this new world.

1 NO BLIND BELIEFS

Close your eyes and imagine standing at the edge of a vast, open field. The air is crisp, the horizon endless. This is your life, free from the stories you've been told about who you are or what you should be.

Now, picture a heavy backpack strapped to your shoulders, filled with rocks—each one a belief you've carried without question. "I'm not smart enough." "I don't deserve love." "All those people are against me."

Feel the weight pressing down, making each step harder. These are blind beliefs you absorbed—unexamined, inherited, and heavy.

They're not yours: they're echoes of voices that never knew your Song.

Letting them go is like dropping that backpack, releasing what was never yours to carry.

You can feel the pressure slip out of your body, your breath deepen. You're lighter now, free to walk your own path, to seek your own truth.

2 NO JUDGMENTS

Imagine sitting by a river, watching the water flow effortlessly over stones, around bends, never stopping to label or condemn. It just moves, accepting each twist and turn.

Now, think of the last time you judged yourself or someone else—"I'm a failure." "They're wrong." "This shouldn't be here." "They shouldn't behave like that."

Feel the tension in your belly, the way it dams your energy like a bolder blocking the river's flow. Judgment and condemnation are walls we build, cutting us off from love, from truth, from each other, from the beauty of what is.

When you release them, the walls crumble. The river of your Song flows freely again, embracing every part of you, every person, every moment.

You're not here to label—you're here to experience, to learn, to love unconditionally. This No No helps us feel the passion of aliveness in our every step.

3 NO EXPECTATIONS

Picture yourself holding a blank canvas, paintbrush in hand. There's no image in your mind, no plan to follow—just pure possibility. This is life without expectations: creative, open, curious, alive.

Now, imagine someone hands you a script, telling you exactly what to paint, how to feel, what to expect. The canvas sags; the colors are washed out.

Expectations are like that script—they box you in, blinding you to the magic of the moment. They whisper, "It should be this way," and when it's not, disappointment follows.

But when you set the script aside, the canvas is fresh, bare. You're free to create, to explore, to be surprised by life's unfolding. You are painting without rules, trusting the brushstrokes of your Song.

Walking our lives without expectations is experiencing the world as it births something new from moment to moment.

4 NO ASSUMPTIONS

Imagine walking through a forest at dawn, the air thick with mist. You can't see far ahead, but each step reveals something new—a flower, a stone, a hidden path. This is life without assumptions: a journey of discovery, where you feel your way forward.

Now, picture yourself striding through that same forest with a map you've drawn from memory, assuming you know every turn. You miss the flower, trip over the stone, and ignore the path.

Assumptions are that map—rigid, outdated, blinding you to what's real. They steal the wonder of the unknown right from under your very feet, replacing it with stale, dull lies.

When you let them go, you notice the wonderful little nuances, sense your connectedness deeply, and feel your Song glowing in love.

5 NO JUMPING TO CONCLUSIONS

Think of a puzzle scattered on a table, pieces waiting to be fit together. If you rush, forcing them into place, the picture distorts. But if you pause, observe, let the shapes guide you, the image emerges naturally. Life is that puzzle.

Jumping to conclusions is like jamming the pieces—driven by fear, impatience, or the need to be right. It warps your view, breeding conflict and confusion.

When you step back, breathe, and let the pieces fall into place, clarity blooms. You see the whole picture, not just the fragments. You are trusting yourself to let your eyes reveal the puzzle, one *patient* piece at a time.

6 NO ARROGANCE

Imagine standing on a mountaintop, the world vast and sprawling below. You feel small, not in a diminishing way, but in awe of the grandeur. This is altruism: knowing you're part of something immense, always learning, always growing.

Now, picture yourself on that same mountain, chest puffed, declaring, "I've seen the same thing before, I know all about that already." The view shrinks; the wonder fades. Arrogance is that puffed chest—it blinds you to the lessons, the beauty, the love waiting in the view.

When you release it, the world speaks. You listen, feel, learn, and expand. Every minute is a wonder and a breath of fresh air.

7 NO NEGATIVE PERCEPTIONS

Picture a garden at twilight, shadows stretching across the flowers. If you focus only on the shadows, you miss the petals, the colors, the aliveness of the moment.

Negative mindsets and perceptions are like that—they zoom in, riding on the dark, blinding you to the light and the miracle of the beauty at hand. They whisper, "Everything's nasty everywhere, it's the way it is, live with it." "This is all there ever is." "Something goes wrong here every time."

When in truth, the garden is blooming with extraordinary magic, diversity and beauty. When you shift your gaze away from the gloom, the shadows change and fade away. You see the beauty, the potential—the magic.

This is the only way to live—walking in beauty with this No No.

CHAPTER 2
THE POWER OF ATTENTION

The Ocean of Consciousness

Picture yourself sitting by a quiet lake at dawn, the water so still it mirrors the sky. The air is calm, the world hushed, and for a moment, you feel completely present—alive, aware, connected. This lake is your consciousness, vast and deep, the source of everything you are.

Now imagine tossing a handful of pebbles into that lake. Ripples spread in every direction, breaking the stillness, scattering your focus. Those pebbles are the thoughts, blind beliefs, and distractions that pull you away from the truth of who you are.

This chapter is about reclaiming that stillness, learning to focus your attention purposefully, and stepping into the sacred power that has always been yours.

We are pure attention—pure awareness—pure consciousness.

Take a moment to feel that—not to think it, not to analyze it—but to feel it.

What does it feel like to be pure attention? It's not a concept to wrestle with; it's a sensation, a subtle, wordless knowing deep within you.

Your consciousness is like a great ocean—endless, alive, the energy of every experience, every thought, every dream. When your attention is stagnant, not focused or engaged, or fostering the growth of deadly things, it's as if the ocean lies dormant, sick. Nothing moves, nothing healthy grows, nothing changes. It's a kind of suspended stagnation, a void where life doesn't unfold.

But when you focus your attention with purpose, the ocean stirs. Waves rise, currents flow, and suddenly, you're creating, learning, experiencing, inspiring life.

This is the power of attention: it's the spark that springs authenticity, aliveness, and beauty into your conscious awareness.

The voice of silence is talking to you.

The Ancient Key

For millennia, the ability to purposefully focus attention has been the heart of all mystical teachings. It's the ancient key to awakening, the secret whispered by shamans, sages, and keepers of wisdom like the Hetakas of Peru and the pre-flood Egyptians. They knew that attention isn't just a tool—*it's who we are—what we are*. It defines the state of our consciousness, showing us where we're clear and where we're stuck. It's the measure of our freedom.

But here's the catch: our modern world has taught us to scatter that attention. From the chatter of our minds to the noise of daily life, we've learned to jump from one thought to the next, our focus fractured by our blind beliefs and old lazy mind habits. Our culture has spent at least a thousand years trying to diminish our consciousness—squelching it, breaking it apart, tossing the pieces far from reach.

We've been trained to have short attention spans, to let our minds be hijacked by masks—like those old stories, "I'm not good enough," or "I can't do this," or "they'll laugh at me."

We've been trained to settle for mediocrity, pacifiers, distractions. These interruptions aren't just annoyances, they're signs of how deeply asleep we are. We've buried our true selves under heaps of mind debris, tossed our way by the upside-down-backwards-turning culture beast.

Have you ever wondered why you don't feel the happiness that's portrayed in the movies? Do you feel "ok" most of the time, a kind of "good enough," but not truly happy on the inside? Are you realizing that the happiness has silently slipped away from you? Are you afraid of living happily all the time or that being successful will make your friends distance themselves from you? Would that make you too different from the rest of the people, that maybe they won't like you or accept you any more? Are you afraid that would make you a target?

What is happiness anyway?

What happened to it?

The Thief in Your Mind

How often does your mind wander? You decide to focus on something—a task, a goal, a moment of peace—and within seconds, a thought bubbles up. Maybe it's a worry, a memory, or a harsh judgment about yourself.

That's the thief at work, the programming beast we've inherited from a culture that thrives on distraction. The more these interruptions happen, the more your consciousness is pushed down, hidden beneath the layers of noise.

But here's the beauty: this isn't permanent. Your consciousness—your Song—can't be destroyed. It's sacred, unbreakable, a piece of the Creator's own awareness living within you. No matter how scattered your attention has become, you can reclaim it. You can learn to focus it, to quiet the thief, to make the beast fade away forever, making it possible for you to feel the stillness of that lake and return home.

There's an old saying that's been passed around through a number of circles that says, "The devil can have my car, my house, my money—*but never my joy!*"

Chea's Circles in the Sand

It was a golden afternoon in Santa Cruz, the sun casting a warm glow over the sandy front yard of the Hetakas' tiny cottage near the beach. The distant crash of waves mingled with the salty breeze, creating a soothing backdrop.

Chea Hetaka, my teacher, sat cross-legged in the sand, her presence as calming as the ocean itself. Her white hair framed a face etched with kindness, and her eyes sparkled with a knowing light.

I sat across from her, fidgeting, my mind a jumble of worries I couldn't get out of my head—school deadlines, a faltering friendship, the nagging sense that I was falling short.

Chea picked up a stick and began tracing a large, smooth circle in the sandy dirt. "This is you," she said, her voice steady and warm. "Your Song, your pure attention, the essence of who you are."

I nodded, intrigued but not knowing where she was going with this.

Then, she drew scraggly lines radiating outward from the circle, each ending in a small, cramped box. "And these," she continued, "are your masks—blind beliefs you've picked up along the way. Like thinking you're not smart enough, or that you're unlovable, or that you've failed as a daughter. This is how you are using your attention today."

Her words pierced me, naming the invisible weights I carried. I felt my neck tighten as I recognized each box as a story I'd clung to, a lie I'd fed with my own energy, since I could remember.

"Look how scattered your attention becomes," she said, gesturing to the many sprawling lines. "You're pouring yourself into these illusions, leaving little attention for what's real."

I thought of my latest school project—a passion I wanted to pursue—but how? I could barely focus, distracted by everything, especially the nagging self-doubt.

Then Chea drew a second big circle, this one untethered and humming with energy.

"This is your Song in its truth," she said. From the big circle she drew a single, bold, wide line to a slightly smaller circle.

"And this is your purpose. Focus your attention like this," tapping the wide line with the new circle, "and your energy is collected, purposeful, aimed, and the beast disappears. You don't feed the beast with your attention and it dies away."

Staring at the sand, I felt a dawning clarity—the exhaustion of chasing false beliefs lifting, replaced by a flicker of possibility. My head felt clearer. Maybe I could reclaim my attention, step by step, and live from my Song.

The Sacredness of You

In the ancient ways, attention is holy, divine, sacred.

The Hetakas don't even have a word for "judgment;" they have no concept of condemning or belittling. They discern—carefully, clearly—but they don't degrade.

Imagine growing up in a world like that, where no one throws dark energy darts at themselves or each other.

What would that feel like?

What kind of life would that be?

Our culture, though, has belittled the sacred. For thousands of years, it's pushed us to dismiss the spiritual, the unseen, the nonlinear—anything that connects us to our true power. This wasn't an accident; it was a way to control us, to keep us away from our own inner knowledge.

But the old teachings, preserved by people like the Hetakas, are rising again. They've been held in secret around the world, passed down through generations, waiting for this time—our time—to be reclaimed.

Your attention is sacred because it is consciousness itself, it's aliveness itself, it's love itself. It's the light of truth shining ubiquitously. It's the fuel behind everything—every thought, every feeling, every atom of existence.

Linear or nonlinear, seen or unseen, it all flows from consciousness. And you? You're a piece of that divine universal consciousness, a unique Song within the Creator's vast symphony.

Reclaiming Your Attention

The following story shows how one woman reclaimed her attention by questioning the lies she'd lived by, discovering the truth of her Song.

Merrian's Realization

Merrian sat cross-legged on the woven rug, her eyes fixed on a point in the air where the morning light seemed to linger. The room was quiet, the echoes of our Song Ceremony fading like ripples on a still pond. Her breath was slow, her face a canvas of wonder and disbelief. For a long moment, she said nothing, as if the world she'd known had paused, suspended in the truth she'd just glimpsed.

Then, in a whisper, she spoke, "I can't believe it… it can't be true…" Her voice trembled, caught in a loop of realization. "I've been living a lie."

Merrian was the picture of success by society's standards. A stellar student, she'd embraced a fierce work ethic, earned a doctorate in psychology, and secured a prestigious job at a college. She'd followed every rule, met every expectation, and chased the approval of her parents, her peers, the world.

Yet, in that sacred moment after the ceremony, as her mind replayed the experience, a truth broke through like dawn through a storm. "The things I thought mattered," she said, her voice cracking, "the achievements, the rules, the institutions—they're not what I thought. They were about *me*—*my* need for approval, for validation, for someone to say I belonged."

She paused, her gaze softening as if seeing herself for the first time. "I never felt truly connected," she admitted. "I was always proving something, chasing a nod from others to feel okay. I believed I had to earn my place, that love and acceptance were rewards for being 'good enough.'

But it was all a story—a lie I told myself, it was all somebody else's lies, their stories."

Merrian's life had been shaped by blind beliefs, those unexamined stories we inherit from family, culture, and society. They told her that success defined her worth, that rules were truth, that love was conditional. She'd poured her attention into this dream, letting it consume her energy, her focus, her very Song—the vibrant, eternal essence of who she truly was.

"The institutions, the systems," she said, shaking her head, "they're just fumbling along. There's no heart in them, no honesty, no beauty. I was so naive."

In the stillness of the ceremony, guided by the ancient wisdom, Merrian had glimpsed the truth. Her attention, once scattered across the demands of a disconnected world, had turned inward. She felt the depths of her Song for the first time—a warm, humming, radiant core that needed no approval, no external measure. It was her birthright, a melody of love, connectedness, and aliveness that had been there all along, hidden beneath the weight of lies.

That moment was her awakening. The ceremony had peeled back the fog, revealing the precarious fantasy she'd mistaken for reality. She saw the world as it was—not a rigid structure of rules, but a living tapestry of beauty, woven with the threads of every Song.

Her attention, once trapped, was now free to dance with this truth. "I'm feeling who I am," she said, a quiet smile breaking through. "I'm remembering—not the story I was told. But my Song—the love, the beauty, the connectedness that's always been inside me."

Merrian's journey is all of ours. Her story reminds us that our attention is sacred, a gift we can reclaim from the lies that have been binding us all. By questioning, feeling, and turning toward our Song, we step into a world alive with possibility—a world where love flows freely, where beauty is not earned but lived.

Today, Merrian teaches others to find their Song, sharing the love she once sought.

So, how do you reclaim your attention, your focus? Start by questioning your beliefs and anything around you. Try noticing one belief today—where does it pull your focus? You can watch—*without judgment*—how your mind works. How long can you focus before a distraction pulls you away? How often do those old masks bubble up, stealing your attention and peace? Don't blame yourself; this is just how we've been taught to live.

But you can unlearn it.

THE 7 NO NOS
AND YOUR
ATTENTION

Your attention is your power—the lens through which you experience the world. The 7 No Nos clean that lens, clearing the distortions that cloud your Song. Here's how each one helps you reclaim your focus.

1 NO BLIND BELIEFS

Imagine your attention as a loud beaming signal, like a lighthouse cutting through the fog to warn the boats that pass by. Blind beliefs are threatening storms that scatter and drown out that sound, dimming its power to help the travelers. They whisper, "Don't look here; don't question this," pulling your focus into the haze.

When you release the blind beliefs, the storms part, the darkness lifts. Your light is seen, and the warning sound is heard clear and strong, telling the story of what's real, what's true.

The boats are no longer lost in the storm; the beauty of the melody of your Song is no longer scattered in the storm, and you are holding the path safe for others to find.

2 NO JUDGMENTS

Picture your attention as a marvelous magic fairy that illuminates everything she looks upon; and judgment and condemnation are bandits that put a black bag over her head and lock her in a deep, dark cellar. She can't illuminate anything but the inside of the black bag.

The bandits say, "That fairy's no good." "She's weak and broken and dangerous." "None of you are any good now either."

When you don't listen to the bandit's judgments anymore—when you stop believing in them—you stop feeding them, and the bandits, black bag and cellar disappear like a fog in the sun.

Your attention surges forward very bright and clear, illuminating everything you perceive, bringing the love, beauty, and magic back into your life and out into the whole of the world.

3 NO EXPECTATIONS

Think of your attention as a dancer, moving gracefully to the music of your Song. Expectations are chains that bind the dancer's feet, forcing rigid steps instead of fluid motion. They murmur, "It must be this way," and the dance falters.

When you release the expectations, the chains fall away, there is self-sovereignty and beauty, not giving your power away to some dictate. Your attention dances freely, twirling with the passion of what is, free to create.

4 NO ASSUMPTIONS

Imagine your attention as a painter's brush, poised to create something new. Assumptions are old sketches that demand where the brush must go, stifling creativity. They insist, "It's always been this way," and the canvas stays deadly dull and ugly.

When you let them go, the brush moves freely. Your attention paints with fresh strokes, revealing beauty you hadn't imagined.

5 NO JUMPING TO CONCLUSIONS

Picture your attention as a gardener, tending to each plant with care. Jumping to conclusions is like yanking up seedlings before they've had a chance to grow, declaring, "This won't work. It should look this way, and feel like this." It kills the potential. When you release this habit, your attention nurtures each moment, letting it bloom in its own time. The garden flourishes, and so do you.

6 NO ARROGANCE

Think of your attention as a cup, always ready to be filled with wisdom. Arrogance acts as a lid that seals the cup, blocking any flow. It boasts, "I'm already full," and learning and sharing stop.

When you remove the lid, your attention becomes like a magic vessel, open to the endless pouring of life's teachings. You drink deeply, and your cup is always overflowing with abundance.

7 NO NEGATIVE PERCEPTIONS

Imagine you are an alien from another planet. Your attention is your antenna, perceiving the paths around you. Negative perceptions are the dirt, twigs, leaves and bugs that got caught on your antenna, distorting and interrupting your perception. They whisper, "This place is all dirty and nasty, but you can't get out of here," and the way seems bleak.

When you unravel and clean your antenna, your attention buzzes with excitement. The path glows with beauty and love, and you can see the truth of the aliveness and possibilities that are all around you and on the paths ahead.

This Is Your Birthright

This is your journey home—to a life where your consciousness is yours to command.

It's not about perfection; it's about awareness, about choosing where to place the gift of your attention. When you focus your attention purposefully, you step into your power. You create, you grow, you awaken, you see the world and yourself as it truly is, and you expand your consciousness.

You are not the distractions.

You are not the masks.

You are not the labels.

You are pure attention, pure consciousness, a sacred piece of Creator. This power belongs to you—not just to some, but to all of humanity.

Welcome it.

Feel it.

Live it!

The world has waited long enough for you to remember.

CHAPTER 3

THE GIFT OF UNCONDITIONAL LOVE

There Is An Endless Ocean Of Love

Picture yourself standing beneath a night sky, stars scattered like countless sparks of light, each one a testament to a force so vast it defies comprehension.

Now imagine that this force isn't just light or energy—it's love. Unconditional love. An endless ocean of love, surging through the cosmos, forming galaxies, solar systems, and the very ground beneath your feet.

This love isn't something you have to chase or earn; it's been here from the beginning, waiting for you to notice. This chapter is about stepping out of the shadows of conditional love and into the boundless embrace of what's real—love without limits, love that simply is. Love that is unconditional.

The Illusion of Scarcity

For thousands of years, humanity has lived in a drought of unconditional love. In our modern world, especially in Western culture, love has been turned into a commodity to barter with, corrupted, defiled. We're taught from a very young age that what our culture calls love, affection, and acceptance comes with a catch. You must behave a certain way, meet certain standards, and never step too far outside the lines—or this so-called love will be taken away.

This is the programming we've inherited, the mask we've worn: a belief that this real love is scarce, a reward to be earned through performance, and giving up your self-sovereignty, your self-respect, and freedom.

This mask tries to cover up a truth too big to hide. Our universe is made of unconditional love—vast, incomprehensible masses of it. Tsunamis of love, a hundred times the size of our galaxy, surge through our solar system and our planet right now, returning to us, calling us home.

But the programming tells us to ignore it, to pretend we don't feel it, offering us conditional love instead—a poor substitute that keeps us tethered to fear and judgment and war.

The Weight of Conditions

Conditional love is a heavy burden. It demands that we conform to others' expectations, that we live up to borrowed pictures of who we're "supposed to be." If we fail, we're pushed away, cast out, or left to face the sting of disapproval—from others and ourselves. We learn to withhold love from our own hearts, condemning ourselves when we don't "measure up."

This isn't love. It's a lonely cage—a self-imposed cage with the door open. It traps us in a cycle of striving for the wrong things, being trapped in hating and fearing, judging and hiding, and disconnecting us from the truth of who we are.

Most of us don't know there's another way. We've been handed this broken box of conditional love and told it's all there is. But the Ka Ta See teachings, carried through ancient traditions, whisper something different: real love has no price. It doesn't demand, judge, or exile. Nor does it fight any wars, large or small. It flows freely and endlessly, like an ocean, to everyone and everything, just as they are.

Tsunamis of Unconditional Love

Unconditional love is the heartbeat of Ka Ta See and the pre-flood Egyptian mysteries. It's what our universe and everything in it is made out of, even you and me and all humanity, all life. It has never diminished or been destroyed—it has only multiplied. It always has been, is, and always shall be.

It's the recognition that every being—every Song—deserves love, no matter who they are, what they've done, or what they believe. This doesn't mean excusing destructive behaviors; it means accepting the essence of each person, their ancient and wondrous Song, without trying to change or control them. It's about loving them anyway, sending loving energy even when it's tough, even when they don't "deserve" it by the world's standards.

Unconditional love lets go of expectations and demands. It doesn't insist that others be different or fit a mold. It sees the homeless person, the guru, and you with the same reverence, knowing each Song is vast, unique, and brimming with love. No one's purpose is ours to dictate—every life unfolds according to its own rhythm, its own beauty.

Acceptance Without Strings

Daniel's story shows how a crisis can awaken us to the harm of conditional love, showing us how this man embraced acceptance without strings.

Daniel's Redemption

Daniel was the kind of man who seemed to have it all. A brilliant mind, a successful career, and a loving family—his wife, Sandy, and their three young children, Bobby, Amy, and Debby—were his pride and joy. He'd followed every rule society laid out: excelled in school, climbed the corporate ladder, and worked long hours at a high-stress job to provide for those he cherished most. Yet, beneath the surface, the weight of that life was eroding him, stress was carving quiet cracks in his heart.

One ordinary day, those cracks became a chasm. Five-year-old Amy fell gravely ill, her back racked with pain and she was unable to keep food down. Daniel and Sandy rushed her to the hospital, fear gripping them like a vice.

"What's wrong with my baby?" Daniel pleaded with the nurse, his voice struggling with worry and guilt.

The hospital's sterile halls offered no answers, only tests and waiting. Days blurred into nights, and nights into days, with Amy's condition unchanged. Sandy urged Daniel to go home, to eat, to rest, but he refused, tethered to his daughter's bedside, his heart heavy with the thought that he'd failed her.

The doctors finally discovered the cause, and she needed surgery immediately. Now utterly exhausted, Daniel wandered the hospital corridors, stumbling into the Meditation Chapel—a small, quiet sanctuary bathed in soft light.

Alone, he sank onto a bench, his body surrendering to a deep, desperate sleep. In that dream, the walls of his life crumbled.

Memories of his childhood flooded into the dream: a stern father, rigid rules, and expectations that left no room for his true self. Affection was withheld when he broke the rules, replaced by silence and distance, his parents wouldn't even look at him or be in the same room with him.

As a boy, he'd learned to appease his parents, to be a people pleaser, to bury and forget his own desires to avoid that searing pain. He'd thought it was normal, he thought he was happy, that everybody lived like that. But now he saw the truth: he'd been terribly lonely, afraid, and perpetually stressed all along.

"Love" as he experienced it, he realized now, had been a transaction to be bought and sold.

The dream turned darker as Daniel saw himself mirroring that pattern with his own children. Rules, expectations, and conditions had crept into his parenting, dimming the light of the children with the same fear and loneliness he'd known.

Amy, his bright, curious little girl, lay in a hospital bed, and he wondered with a pang, "What are her dreams? Do I even know her heart?"

The thought that she might slip away, having known only his rules and not his boundless love, broke him.

"This isn't love," he whispered in his dream, tears staining his cheeks. "It's 'power over other', it's cruelty. We wouldn't treat a stray dog this way."

In the chapel's peace, a revelation stirred in his restless dream. "Where did these reactions come from?" His mind tracing the pattern back through generations— his parents, their parents, their parents before them, a legacy of conditional love stretching across time.

"I have to stop this!" he vowed, his voice fierce with resolve. "I have to free my family, free myself. I can't even tell who I am. We need love without strings—no rules, no conditions, no demands, just pure love that's felt, given, and received, always."

Sandy found him there, her touch gentle as she woke him.

Dazed, he mumbled, "We need unconditional love, Sandy. For the kids, for us. No more rules, no more fear, no more stress."

Before she could respond, the doctors entered with a miracle: Amy was ok. She would recover, stronger than ever. Relief washed over Daniel, but his resolve held firm.

That day, he quit his soul-draining job, choosing a simpler path—a small business with room for joy. He set out to discover his own Song, to learn his children's dreams, and to weave a home where love flowed freely, unburdened by conditions.

Daniel's story is a mirror for us all. Conditional love is a cage we've all known, but unconditional love—acceptance without strings—is our birthright.

By giving up the conditions and rules and embracing the truth of our Songs, we can heal, feel our deep connectedness, and live in the beauty of what is. Let Daniel's courage inspire you to love without limits, starting today.

Notice a moment today where you impose conditions on love. Can you offer acceptance instead, feeling the freedom it brings you and others? Can you do it again, and again?

Unconditional acceptance walks hand in hand with unconditional love. It's the gentle act of seeing truthfully what something actually is—yourself, others, the world—without resistance, or labeling, or judging, or lying to yourself. In the Ka Ta See way, unconditional acceptance isn't bending to fear or being overpowered. It isn't about condoning bad behavior.

Unconditional acceptance is clarity, an expression of real love; it's acknowledging a bigger picture. It's wanting to let go of the weight you've been carrying; letting go of the "shoulds" and old lies that cloud your vision—and embracing each moment as part of the greater tapestry.

When you accept yourself without conditions, you stop battling your own Song. You release the masks and step into your truth. When you accept others as they are, you lift the weight of judgment from both of you. This is where freedom begins, where love can flow unchecked.

THE 7 NO NOS
AS A PATH TO LOVE

Love is the wave upon wave of creation that floods all of existence for eternity—it floods your Song and all Songs. Love is the essence of awakening. The 7 No Nos clear the barriers to love, opening you to its boundless flow. Here's how each one guides you toward unconditional love.

1 NO BLIND BELIEFS

Love is like the light that radiates from all things because everything is alive. Blind beliefs are storms of smoke, clouds, ash, poisons, dirt and dust that cover the light. They say, "That kind of love doesn't exist," and "Love must be earned," or "I'm not worthy of love," and the people suffer in the darkness.

When you release the blind beliefs, the storms die away. Love flows freely, unconditionally, shining over you and through you, through everything, flooding you with the rays of All That Is.

2 NO JUDGMENTS

Love is a bridge, and judgment is a wall that divides and blocks the bridge, there is no circulation, no giving and receiving, no communication, no flow on the roadway. The wall labels, separates, and says, "You're not like me." "You can't be on my side of the bridge."

When you let it go, the wall falls. Love rebuilds the bridge, Song to Song, heart to heart. You see the other is just like you in so many ways, and the connection is born and deepens as time rolls on.

3 NO EXPECTATIONS

Love is a gift, and expectations are strings attached. They demand, "Be this way," and then love becomes a lopsided bartering war.

When you release them, the strings snap. Love is given freely, received freely, a dance of beauty and grace without demands.

4 NO ASSUMPTIONS

Love is a conversation, and assumptions are unspoken words that distort the message. They whisper, "I know what you mean," or "It has to be done this way," and misunderstanding grows.

When you let them go, the conversation clears. Love speaks truthfully, listens deeply, and the bond strengthens.

5 NO JUMPING TO CONCLUSIONS

Love is the most powerful, soothing, connecting, peaceful, healing energy in our universe. It creates friendships, communication, sharing, gratefulness, forgiveness....and the list goes on and on. It creates all life and all consciousness. Everything!

But humans are a very young race in the cosmos and they can get fooled very easily. One day, a very long time ago by human standards, a group of humans were sitting around a fire talking about some friends who recently died, when a whirlwind stirred up. One of them jumped to conclusions, saying it was their friends coming back to scare them; they all believed it and ran away.

The story spread fast and grew from tribe to tribe until even today, many people believe that story and are frightened by it. They still have not stopped long enough to see and feel the real truth.

Ghosts are not the dead coming back to frighten or hurt anybody. What the people are sensing has nothing to do with the Songs of the dead. Ghosts are just the temporary energetic forms of thoughts and emotions that have been created by all of us humans.

When we jump to conclusions, we miss the real, often more spectacular show altogether.

6 NO ARROGANCE

Love creates living human systems that can be represented by a circle with a dot in the center—this is showing us a Song—a living human. The dot in the center represents the spiritual non-linear aspect, and the ring around the dot is the material, physical aspect, making a space for the spiritual.

If arrogance crowds in and takes over the central spot, all forms of chaos ensue, and the spiritual is shoved out of the picture. Priorities go upside-down-and-backwards.

When the spiritual is in the center and the circle is around the dot, the person is in balance and harmony with the universe—the spiritual is the center of the human's life, energy and information. It is the source of love, peace, connectedness, happiness, abundance, beauty, harmony, intelligence, information, expanding consciousness…. *and life itself.*

Life fulfills what creation intended it to.

7 NO NEGATIVE PERCEPTIONS

Love is a great, huge, glorious dragon that glows and sparkles like starlight. It is love personified, wise and kind. It's magic itself. It can live in and move through the earth and rock, no matter how deep....It can live and move on the surface of the land with ease....The dragon can live in and swim through the waters....It can live in and move through fire with no harm....It can live in and fly through the sky and heaven as naturally as can be....It can live in and travel through the mystical ethers as the ethers do, traveling from location to location in an instant....It has access to all the information of the world, sees the past and sees where the future is leading.

One day, a fog moved in and covered the land of the humans and they could no longer hear the dragon's golden words of love and assistance; they only saw a dark and looming figure of something they couldn't understand. The fog was numbing, inebriating. The people were conned, told lies about the dragon and love and magic. They lost their way, addicted to the fog. Life became miserable and ugly.

The fog said the dragon was bad, horrible, dangerous for all, that they would have to catch it and hide it far away in a dark space. So the fog told the people to make a huge, strong net and capture the dragon and bury it. And they did.

The fog is like negative perceptions that suck the magic, love, happiness and beauty out of your heart and mind, and your life and world so that you can no longer feel love and its magic and beauty, let alone live by it.

When you challenge the fog of blind beliefs, you unbury the beautiful dragon—the love—the magic and adventure of life are yours to live as you see fit, in beauty and love forever.

PRACTICE 1

SENDING LOVE
WITHOUT CONDITIONS

Here's a simple way to begin: pick someone—
anyone, even someone you find difficult—and
send them love. No strings, no expectations,
no need for them to respond or change.
Picture a warm, gentle light moving from your
heart to theirs. Do this silently, without words
or interactions—just send it out and let it be.

You might see a change in them—a softening,
a spark. Or maybe the shift happens in you—a
lightness, a sense of peace. It doesn't matter
what they do with it. The act of giving love
without conditions is its own reward, a quiet
revolution in the Songs of the world.

The Truth of Your Song

Every Song—yours, mine, everyone's—is born from unconditional love and overflows with it. It's the nature of life itself. The masks we wear can't erase it; this ocean is too deep, too persistent, and deliciously ubiquitous. As you walk the path of the 7 No Nos, you'll feel it more and more—the love that's been waiting for you to claim.

This is how Ka Ta See sees the world: through eyes of love and acceptance, giving love freely without keeping score. It's not always simple, but it's the way back to your Song, the beauty, the endless ocean that holds us all.

Step Into the Ocean

You're not the cracked cup of conditional love. You're not the programming that's kept you small. You are the ocean—ancient, vast, powerful, and full of love. This chapter invites you to step in, to release the old stories, and to let love flow through you without hesitation. As it does, you'll see the world change—not because it has to, but because love transforms everything it touches.

Keep this love close as you move forward. Let it guide you, lift you, and remind you of your true nature. The drought is over. The ocean is calling.

PART TWO
THE WATER IN THE DESERT

CHAPTER 4

THE POWER OF QUESTIONING

The Prison of Blind Beliefs

We live in a culture that hands us a madman's box of beliefs—ideas we've collected from family, society, and media, hoarding them like treasures without ever asking if they're true. These blind beliefs are data we've accepted without scrutiny, charged with emotions like fear or arrogance, shaping how we see ourselves and the world. They tell us we're not smart enough, that life is a struggle, that separation is real. But they're lies, masking the truth of our Song and the haunting beauty that flows through all things.

Why It Matters

Blind beliefs keep us asleep, trapped in a pretend world. They suck away our power, making us victims of someone else's bad story. The ancients taught that to awaken, we must *question everything!*—every thought, every assumption, every so-called "truth" we've swallowed whole.

As kids we never learned about questioning—and that has made us victims—gullible, weak and afraid. Questioning isn't about cynicism; it's about reclaiming your sovereignty, peeling away the mud-glopped lenses to see reality as it is: ancient, vast, alive with love, and brimming with a beauty that's mind-blowing in its scope.

When we let go of these beliefs, we open our senses to the "water in the desert" that has been all around us all the time.

There it is….what we have all been looking for, for millennia—the banquet of the universe—the mysteries that empower our awareness—how delicious and sacred our connectedness is—the magic in the dance and love of "ordinary" aliveness….

There it is….the beauty of love.

Sarah's Story

Sarah's palms were sweaty as she stood at the edge of the small Toastmasters room, her heart hammering with a fear she'd carried since high school. She could still see it: standing before her English class at sixteen, her voice trembling as she read a poem, only to be met with snickers and a teacher's dismissive wave.

The humiliation had seared into her, shaping a belief that she was hopeless at public speaking. For years, she shrank from any chance to speak, her voice silenced by that single, defining moment.

It was her friend Mia who nudged her toward change. "Just try one meeting," Mia urged, her enthusiasm infectious. Sarah resisted, but a quiet question stirred within her, "What if that old story isn't true?"

She arrived at Toastmasters with her stomach in knots, taking a seat in the back. The room buzzed with warmth—people of all ages chatting, laughing, preparing to speak. When it was her turn to introduce herself, her voice cracked, but no one mocked her. Instead, they clapped, their smiles genuine.

Over the weeks, Sarah kept returning, each visit a small act of courage. She learned to breathe through her nerves and to organize her thoughts, but the real shift came from questioning her belief. "Am I really terrible at this?" she wondered, testing the evidence. With every shaky sentence, every nod of encouragement, the answer softened.

Then came her first full speech—a story of her journey from silence to voice. She stood tall, her words flowing, and when she finished, the applause washed over her like a tide. Tears rolled from her eyes, not from shame, but from liberation. By doubting one belief, she'd cracked open a door to her Song, reclaiming a piece of herself she'd thought lost.

In that moment, she felt the beauty of her own courage—a passion and peace woven into her being—and saw the beauty of a community that held space for her growth, a reflection of the universe's banquet unfolding before her.

PRACTICE 2

UNCOVERING YOUR BLIND BELIEFS

When we do practices and ceremonies, these are sacred activities, you are creating "sacred space." That means we always make sure we are in a quiet space where we will not be interrupted, or distracted by the noises and sounds of others. We make sure that we have plenty of time for everything we want to work on and that the space is comfortable.

Feel into how fortunate you are to have this sacred opportunity to awaken to a deeper, ancient part of yourself. In this space, you want to set the intention to remember, to not get stuck in analytical thinking and words, to stay focused on your task and its goal, and feel with everything that you are.

LIST YOUR BELIEFS

Find a quiet space where you can settle in, maybe with a cup of tea or under a soft blanket. Close your eyes if it feels right, and let your mind drift like a gentle stream.

What stories do you carry about yourself—about your worth, your talents, your role in the world? Write down five beliefs that feel heavy or constricting, like "I'll never be enough," or "I can't trust anyone."

Don't force them; let them bubble up naturally, as if they're surfacing from deep water. Notice how they feel in your body—do they sit like stones in your stomach or a fog in your chest?

How does questioning these beliefs change how you see yourself, your day, your world?

TRACE THEIR ROOTS

Take one belief at a time and travel back with it. Ask "Where did this begin?" Was it a parent's hurried words, a teacher's red pen, a message whispered by the world around you? Picture that moment or person vividly—see their face, hear their tone. Was it spoken from love, fear, or something else? Tune into your body: does your throat tighten, your shoulders hunch?

This is your Song nudging you, hinting at the truth beneath the story. Let the memory unfold without rushing it.

QUESTION THEM

Now, become a gentle detective. For each belief, challenge them, ask, "Is this absolutely true? What proof do I have for it—or against it? What if it's just a shadow, not the light?" Don't judge yourself; let curiosity lead. Feel the shift as you poke at the story—does your chest loosen or your mind brighten? Maybe a small smile creeps in.

This is the old tale unraveling, making space for something truer. Is there something glimmering on the horizon?

FEEL THE SHIFT

As you question your beliefs, pay attention to what moves inside you. Is there a tug of resistance, like a knot twisting in your gut, or a wave of relief, like a breeze lifting a curtain? This is your Song stirring, reclaiming its rhythm. Notice your body: does your spine straighten or your breath grow fuller?

These are quiet signs of coherence building, of coming home to yourself.

RELEASE AND REFRAME

Let go of the beliefs that weigh you down. Picture them dissolving into the Field of Awareness—the vast, loving energy that surrounds and permeates everything—like mist fading in sunlight.

In their place, feel a new truth: "I am enough," or "I can learn to trust." Say it out loud, letting the words vibrate in your chest, your throat, your bones. Feel the energy shift—lighter, brighter, more alive—like a bird taking flight.

EMBRACE THE BEAUTY

Pause and savor the beauty of this freedom. Feel the passion of breaking free, the relief of seeing clearly. Look around: do the colors of your room pop a little more? Do the sounds of life sharpen?

This is the universe's banquet of unconditional love opening before you, its richness revealed as you shed the old. Let it fill you as you catch these steps of becoming awake.

TAKE IT DEEPER

Grab whatever you would like to use to express yourself with. This is the part where you search through your feelings, experiences and reactions and let them all spill out where you can see them right in front of you—face to face.

Write, type, draw, scribble, or doodle. Use crayons, paint, make poetry, carve, make music, sculpt, collage, anything—*just feel and describe*. Tell what happened in those hidden places inside.

No one has to see it but you. Go with the *feeling* of it. This is a mirror of your secret world inside. Don't overthink it. *Feel it.* If there are words, don't edit anything.

This is your Song singing and whispering its secrets to you—*carefully listen and feel*.

CHAPTER 5

LIFE WITHOUT CONDEMNING

The Weight of Judgment

Our culture trains us to judge—ourselves, others, even the toilet paper we don't buy. We fling energy darts of condemnation, labeling things good or bad, better or worse.

My teachers, the Hetakas, had no word for "judgment" in their language. They lived in discernment, observing without the sting of hierarchy.

Judgment stems from blind beliefs, pulling us from our Song into a fog of separation. This No No is called "No Judgements."

Why It Matters

When we judge, we close our hearts, missing the beauty and love flowing through all things. Condemnation isolates us and only gives us loneliness, while discernment lets us know we are connected. It's the difference between cursing a poisonous plant and honoring it as part of creation, as the Hetakas did on their jungle walks. To awaken, we must trade judgment for curiosity, feeling the truth beneath the surface. Discernment unveils the beauty in all things—the unimaginable splendor of every Song, a tsunami of sacredness woven into the Great Field with love by Neith.

The Car Ride Revelation

Years ago, when my kids were tiny—this was before seat belts and kids' car seats—I had to go on an errand, bringing the kids and a close friend. The car hummed along the roadway, my toddlers' giggles from the back seat filling the air as they waved their toys—a plastic dinosaur and a tattered teddy.

It should have been a joyful sound, but I was a knot of tension, my hands had a death grip on the wheel. It was really hot in the car, the traffic was stalled, and the day felt like a runaway train. Then my daughter threw one shoe and one sock sailing out the open window, landing somewhere under a car.

I lost it. "What is wrong with you?" I yelled, my voice a harsh echo of my father's temper.

The laughter just increased.

I started to yell again.

Michael, my friend in the passenger seat, placed a hand on my leg.

"You don't have to do that," he said. "You don't have to be angry or say that," his tone soft, but hit hard.

His words cut through my rage, and I felt a jolt—like waking from a dream. The anger that had burned in my chest just disappeared.

And I saw something else that was hidden. In the mask I'd put on, I was judging my children, expecting them to obey, believing their chaos reflected my failure as a mother. In their wide eyes, I saw myself not as a nurturer, but becoming a source of fear, just like my father. I swore I'd never do that.

The traffic was stopped dead, the engine idling as I turned to them. The kids' chaos melted into the background as they continued to jump up and down, hysterically laughing. My inherited mask of judgment spiced with anger slipped, revealing a truth: my children weren't problems to solve; they were Songs to cherish.

From that moment, I promised to meet them—and myself—with understanding, not criticism, letting love guide me back to my center.

In this shift, I felt the beauty of their innocence, the excitement in their joy, and the peace of accepting them as they are: a glimpse of the universe's banquet, rich with variety and love.

PRACTICE 3
CULTIVATING NON-JUDGMENT

When we do practices and ceremonies, these are sacred activities, you are creating "sacred space," and today we are looking into discernment.

Make sure you are in a quiet space where you will not be interrupted and you have plenty of time for everything you want to work on. With gratitude, feel how healing it is to have created this space, this time, this moment for yourself—steps toward awakening. Set your intention to remember, don't get stuck in analytical thinking and words, stay focused on your task and its goal, and *feel* with everything you are.

CATCH A JUDGMENT

Next time a judgment slips out—like "They're so lazy" or "This is unfair"—stop right there. Take a slow breath and hold the thought gently, like catching a butterfly. Where do you feel it in your body? A tightness in your shoulders, a clench in your jaw? This is the mask of judgment settling in, dimming your light.

FEEL IT

Dive into the emotion fueling that judgment. Is it irritation, a need to feel better-than, or maybe fear? Don't shove it away—let it bloom fully, like a storm passing through. How does it shift your energy—does it shrink you or weigh you down?

This is the thief sneaking in, trying to steal your peace. Sit with it, breathing through it.

SHIFT TO DISCERNMENT

Now, soften your gaze and ask, "What's really going on here? What can I learn instead of labeling?" Drop the "good" or "bad" and seek the heart of it. Feel into the situation with kindness, challenge that judgment—what's the deeper truth? As understanding replaces the snap of judgment, notice your energy lift and your heart open, as understanding replaces the old addiction.

SEND LOVE

Instead of firing an energy dart, offer a quiet gift. Picture a warm golden light flowing from your heart to theirs—or to the moment itself. Feel it soften your edges and melt the tension. This is your Song rising, weaving love where division stood. How does your body feel now—warmer, steadier?

EMBRACE THE BEAUTY

Look for the beauty here. It's the thrill of learning and growing, the peace of letting go. It might be a small thing, like a stranger's patience, a bird's song, or life's unexpected grace. Beauty is attention, our awareness searching for truth, for something more, something coming next— beauty is Song, vast ancient consciousness, copiously rich with memory and knowingness— beauty is love, from the subtle wisp of a rose on the breeze to breath-tingling bliss. Feel your connection to it all. Let it sink in—it's a taste of the universe's banquet, rich with lessons of aliveness and what it means to be human.

TAKE IT DEEPER

Grab whatever you would like to use to express yourself with, and it's time to play. Show how it felt and still feels. What was the experience of moving from judgment to discernment like? Did your old view turn a cartwheel? What beauty peeked through the cracks? Feel your gratitude guide you, honoring this movement toward connectedness and beauty.

CHAPTER 6

THE TRAP OF PRECONCEIVED NOTIONS

Letting Go of Expectations

Pre-scripting is making expectations. They are blind beliefs projected forward, scripting reality before it unfolds. They're like designing an experiment to prove what you already think you "know," blinding you to the present.

In Ka Ta See, we seek truth without preconceptions, open to the vastness of our Song and the world's aliveness. Expectations box us in; letting go sets us free, inviting the unpredictable beauty of the moment—a banquet of variety and flavors.

It's the tsunami of waking up surging through the cosmos.

Why It Matters

When we expect, we miss what's real—love, beauty, connectedness, surprises—replacing it with a pre-programmed story that fits in a stuffy pre-programmed box. Polla, a friend studying Egyptian teachings, expected spirit sight to mimic physical vision. When spirit sight suddenly flooded her, she was overwhelmed and recoiled. Expectations block or warp our spirit senses; openness invites them to awaken, allowing the beauty of the unknown to reveal itself.

Polla's Gift

Polla sat across from me, her brow furrowed with frustration.

"Everyone else sees things," she said, her voice edged with defeat.

"Visions, colors, guides—I just get darkness."

She'd tried every meditation others had suggested, desperate to unlock the vivid spiritual sight she thought her friends described. The absence of spirit sight convinced her she was flawed, that she didn't have any gift. I saw the burden she carried and suggested a completely different approach; I hoped it might shift her perspective and beliefs.

A few days later, she said, "It's happening," her voice trembling. It turns out, as it's commonly referred to—her "third eye had opened"—flooding her day and night with images and sounds, nice and not nice—swirling symbols, faces, shapes, colors, emotions—a kaleidoscope of images on top of images.

It overwhelmed her; she was completely unprepared for seeing the sudden truth of her masks and beliefs that she still held on to. She gripped my hand,

"Make it stop," she pleaded.

I suggested a long sweat lodge with hot rocks and no one else there, just her, and lots of singing sacred songs and asking the spirits to help her.

After the sweat lodge was done, outside, under the cool night sky, she exhaled shakily, "I thought I wanted that, but that was too much."

I smiled. "Your gift isn't spiritual sight, Polla—it's knowingness. This is more important. You feel truths others miss. You pick up the wordless, sightless energy that comes before and underneath the pictures or thoughts—that's the energy that holds all the knowledge and power, the energy that makes the pictures. Your Song was showing you a movie of the masks you still carry."

As the surprising realization slowly sank in, her eyes lit up. She'd been chasing someone else's path, blind to her own strength: an intuitive clarity that needed no visuals or sounds.

From then on, she leaned into that gift, grateful for its quiet power, her Song shining through her acceptance. In releasing her expectation, she embraced the beauty of her unique path—feeling the sacredness of her truth and the serenity of self-acceptance, woven into her being by the power of her own Song.

PRACTICE 4
RELEASING EXPECTATIONS

It is time to build and step into your sacred space. Creating this space with no distractions and no interruptions should become an easeful habit the more times you do it. You are building a spiritual space as you are building physical space; this is a sacred task. Don't get stuck in analytical thinking and words; don't let your whispering masks distract you. Always hold the intent to remember, stay focused on your task and its goal, and feel with everything that you are.

SPOT AN EXPECTATION

Catch yourself predicting something—like "They won't show up" or "This day's ruined." Pause and name it, no shame needed. Where does it settle in your body—a racing pulse, a heavy chest? Feel how letting go of that expectation changed your experience.

This is the weight of expectation pressing down, pulling you from your Song, and the current moment you are living in.

QUESTION IT

Dig a little: "Why do I expect this? Is it rooted in reality or just old echoes?" Think back—did a past letdown or worry sow this seed? Feel its energy: is it shielding you or boxing you in? Let the question hang there, softening the grip of the "should."

FEEL THE PRESENT

Bring yourself back with your senses. What do you see—your room, a flower, a splash of color? What do you hear—a hum, a distant laugh? Touch something—the smoothness of a table, the warmth of your skin. Smell—is the air sweet, or musky? Feel your own bones in your feet. This is your Song rooting you here, in this alive moment.

LET GO

Exhale that expectation, seeing it drift off like a leaf on a river. Open your hands—literally— and welcome whatever comes. Trust the flow, even if it's messy. Feel your body unwind— shoulders easing, breath slowing—as you step into freedom.

EMBRACE THE BEAUTY

Feel the beauty of not knowing—the thrill of surprise, how letting go can be so satisfying. The moment sparkles more now, doesn't it? Like the universe is weaving a tapestry, and you're part of its creation dance. Let that wonder fill you, a sip from the Field of Beauty.

LET'S REFLECT ON THE EXPERIENCE

Grab whatever you would like to use to express yourself with. You are holding the story of what you just examined and questioned—it changed your insides—in what way, can you feel it? What happened with you? What beauty bloomed in the space you made toward freeing yourself?

Express without restraint.

Try feeling without any words—let the different feelings describe the sensations, challenges and realizations.

CHAPTER 7

THE TRAP OF ASSUMPTIONS

Lazy Thinking's Lie

Assumptions are shortcuts born from blind beliefs, a lazy mind's way of avoiding clarity. We assume we know others' thoughts, the world's workings, even our own limits, building walls where bridges could stand.

In Ka Ta See, we feel before we think, letting truth emerge from experience, not guesswork. Feeling truth uncovers the beauty of authentic connection—the electric dance of Songs meeting, a haunting splendor in the Web of Life.

Why It Matters

Assumptions disconnect us from our Song and the Songs of others, fostering isolation over unity. They're the arrogance of disconnection, guessing what's there, what's true, shutting out love and understanding. Real connectedness—Song to Song—requires us to drop the false script and feel what's actually there, revealing the beauty of what truly is:

> *"the beauty of self and the beauty of other."*

The Neighbor's Dog

The barking started at dawn, a relentless yapping that pierced John's morning stillness. For weeks, it had been his nemesis, the neighbor's dog, sabotaging his attempts at meditation. He'd glare out the window, imagining an indifferent owner who didn't care about the noise. His irritation festered, turning into a narrative of blame that colored his days.

One morning, fed up, he decided to try something new. He closed his eyes and reached out with his heart, seeking the dog's energy instead of cursing it. What he felt wasn't defiance—it was loneliness, an aching call for companionship.

John's anger dissolved, replaced by a pang of empathy. He pulled on his shoes and walked next door, knocking softly. An older man answered, his face tired. "I'm sorry about the barking," he said before John could speak. "His brother died last month, and he's been lost without him."

Guilt washed over John—he hadn't known. They talked, and John offered to walk the dog sometimes, to ease his solitude. The man's eyes softened with relief. Later, as John petted the dog's scruffy head, his tail wagged, and the barking took on a new tone—not a nuisance, but a bridge.

John's assumption had built a wall; feeling the truth had torn it down, revealing the power of understanding over judgment. In that connection, he felt the beauty of compassion—the connectedness of feeling and the sacred gift of seeing another's Song.

PRACTICE 5
CHALLENGING ASSUMPTIONS

You are very lucky to have this sacred opportunity to wake up! It's time again to build your special space.

Turn off and tune out everything, everything in the outside world, and everything babbling in your inside world. Relax. Make sure your space is comfortable. This is not a race to get through all the practices below.

Your sacred space is your time to find the peace and beauty of diving into and learning more about yourself. Stay focused on your task and its goal, and act with the intent to remember. Don't get stuck in analytical thinking and words—*feel* with everything that you are.

NOTICE AN ASSUMPTION

When you catch yourself guessing—like "They don't care" or "This won't work"—stop! Challenge your own assumptions! Call it out softly, like spotting a cloud in the sky. Where does it land in you—a twist in your gut, a fog in your head? This is the old programming story sneaking in, pretending to be fact. Whenever we assume we are adding another brick to the prison walls we have learned to encase ourselves in, making its walls thicker and stronger.

PAUSE

Ask: "Do I know this for certain? What's my evidence?" Let the question linger, creating a little pocket of stillness. Feel your body respond—does your breath ease, your mind unclench? This is the space where truth can finally breathe.

FEEL INSTEAD

Close your eyes for a moment and tune into your heart. What's the real energy here— tension, warmth, something else? Let your intuition whisper, cutting through the noise of the mind. Feel beyond the surface—what's alive beneath *that surface?*

ACT FROM TRUTH

Move forward with what you sense, not what you guessed. Maybe it's a kind word, a question, or just listening. Feel into this experience. This is your Song becoming coherent with what's real, building bridges instead of walls.

EMBRACE THE BEAUTY

Notice the beauty in this truth—the spark of understanding, the comfort of clarity. Feel the light of love tying you to this moment, this person, this life. It's the Web of Life glowing, a piece of the universe's banquet laid bare.

LET'S PEEL AWAY THE LAYERS

Grab whatever you would like to use to express yourself with. Create the story of your experience with challenging your own assumptions. What did challenging that assumption feel like?

There are subtle changes inside you with this bold action—once you experience them, you can never *un-experience* them, just like once you see a picture you can't *un-see* it. The magic of the challenging keeps bubbling up—you started the ball rolling.

Approach it with feeling gratitude, honoring this step into sovereignty and love. It's sacred.

CHAPTER 8
AVOIDING RASH CONCLUSIONS

The Leap to Nowhere

Jumping to conclusions is a reckless leap from feeling and exploring to fabrication, fueled by impatience and masks. This rashness is not about the truth of anything. It only distorts reality into a battlefield of confusion and mistrust.

The ancients urged patience and searching, letting understanding unfold naturally. Patience calls for *feeling* the truth, reaching out for beauty, allowing passion to grow, and finding what is actually present—a cosmic force we find in our Song.

Why It Matters

Rash conclusions bury love and beauty, feeding fear and division. They steal us from the present, where real connectedness lives. We always choose what step to take next. This "No No" calls us to grow up, to snap out of the spell, and to let aliveness show us its own truth.

The Wolf Story

The fire glowed in the stillness of the night, casting shadows on the grandfather's weathered face as he sat with his grandson. The boy, wrapped in a blanket, gazed up at him, his dark eyes bright with curiosity. "Grandpa, how do I grow up strong and good?" he asked, his voice a whisper against the crackling logs.

The grandfather's lips curved into a gentle smile.

"Inside you live two wolves," he said. "One is warm and wise, full of kindness and patience. The other is fierce and restless, quick with anger and rash words. They battle every day for your heart."

The boy tilted his head, captivated. "Which one wins?" he asked.

"The one you feed," the grandfather replied.

"Every choice you make," said the grandfather, "every thought, every deed—gives strength to one wolf or the other. Speak with love, and the good wolf grows.

Lash out in haste and unkindness, and the bad wolf thrives."

The boy frowned, puzzled. "But how do I choose right?"

The grandfather rested a hand on the boy's shoulder. "Listen from here," he said, tapping the boy's chest. "The good wolf's voice is soft but steady; the bad wolf's is loud but empty. You'll know."

The boy stared into the flames, picturing the wolves within, and vowed to feed the one that would guide him toward kindness and wisdom. In that vow, he felt the beauty of the sacred—the gentle passion of growth and the peace of choosing well.

PRACTICE 6
PATIENCE IN ACTION

Welcome back to your sacred space! Make sure you are in a quiet area where you won't be disturbed or interrupted. Set aside plenty of time for your practices. Keep moving your focus back on your task and its goal. Do every step with the intent to remember. Don't get stuck in analytical thinking and words—*feel* with everything that you are—*feel*—*feel*—*feel*.

CATCH THE LEAP—STOP JUMPING TO CONCLUSIONS

When you're deciding fast, on an impulse—like "They're mad at me!" or "This is never going to work!"—freeze—notice that urge to leap.

Can you feel you're reacting on autopilot? The rush—heart pounding, hands tensing? This is your mind trying to be the boss, racing ahead—and leaving your Song behind.

BREATHE

Slow it down with a deep inhale, then a long exhale. Let your breath pull you back, like an anchor dropping into calm water. Feel your feet on the floor, your hands still. Your center is calling you home.

OBSERVE

Look closer—what's actually happening? Catch the details: a tone, a glance, the bigger picture. Let curiosity take over, gathering the pieces like a puzzle. Feel your energy getting steady as more light brightens the picture.

CHOOSE

Decide from this clear place, not the rush. Maybe you take action, maybe you wait—whatever feeds kindness, wisdom, love and beauty. Notice how your body feels—grounded, balanced—as you act with care instead of haste.

You always have a choice. Always.

EMBRACE THE BEAUTY

Feel the beauty of this patience—the nuances of life unfolding, the peace of staying present in the calm. The moment deepens, doesn't it? Like the universe's banquet revealing its flavors slowly, richly.

Let it sink in.

TAKE IT DEEPER

Let what you experienced flow out as you express this event. Did pausing change the story? What was waiting there underneath your impatience, behind your mask? Can you sense your Song now?

CHAPTER 9
KEEP THE IKTA OUT

The Illusion of "IKTA"

Arrogance, or "IKTA" (I Know That Already), is the mask of "better-than," a fragile shield always covering the mask of "less-than." It closes off your cup to new wisdom, cutting you from the endless learning Ka Ta See offers.

Being genuinely grateful and humble opens you to the vastness of your Song and the universe's gifts. This No No is embracing the beauty of not-knowing—there's passion in the discovery, and no wars in the humbleness.

This is what waking up weaves into all our lives.

Why It Matters

Arrogance isolates, while being unpretentious connects. It's the difference between Socrates's "I know that I know nothing" and a know-it-all's empty boasts. To awaken, we must shed the lie that we've "arrived," embracing the adventure of not knowing and the beauty, the excitement it reveals.

The Perfume Lesson

My collection of scented oils and lotions was a small but loved indulgence—jasmine, lavender, rose—each bottle a promise of comfort. I'd never thought twice about them until my teacher, a woman of few words but deep insight, asked me about them.

"Why do you use those?" she asked, her tone curious yet pointed. I shrugged.

"They smell nice."

She nodded slowly. "They also cloud your senses—your taste, your smell, your connection to what's real. Those so-called pretty smells are changing your cells. They are engineered to control you, to make you a smiling, stupid slave."

Her words hit me in places I didn't know I had. I loved those scents—surely they couldn't harm me.

But doubt crept in, and I decided to experiment, setting the products aside. Days later, I noticed a change. Coffee tasted richer, the air carried hints of grass and rain I'd missed before. The bread I'd once savored now smelled harsh and unpleasant.

My senses woke up, as if a fog had lifted. I had been numbing myself to the world's subtle beauty and my arrogance concealing the cost. In letting go, I understood, and I felt a quiet gratitude for the lesson—even my Song was humming clearer without the clutter.

In being unpretentious, I was able to embrace the beauty of not knowing—I found passion in discovering, and mostly, the sovereignty of letting the beliefs go.

PRACTICE 7
EMBRACING HUMBLENESS

It's time to look at the elusive IKTA up close. Get settled and quiet in your sacred space. Keep re-focusing your attention back on your task and its goal of waking up out of the programming. Take every step with the intent to remember. Don't get stuck in analytical thinking and words—*feel* with everything that you are—*feel*—*feel*—*feel!*

SPOT THE "I KNOW THAT ALREADY"

Catch the "I know it all" moment—like "I've got this figured out." Pause and feel it—name it. Does it puff you up or wall you off, or both? This is Mr. Slippery Slimy Arrogance slipping in, masking your Song with a false out-of-tune note.

QUESTION EVERYTHING

Ask "What might I miss if I stop here? What else could I learn here?" Let the questions crack your shell, making room for more. Feel your energy soften—less rigid, more open—as being unpretentious tiptoes in.

LISTEN

Step into the moment fresh, like it's your first time. What's new—a tone, a feeling, a detail? Hear it with your heart, not your head. Notice what you'd have skipped before—it's like finding a glowing treasure.

GRATITUDE

Say thank you—to the person, the situation, the lesson—silently or better yet, face to face, out loud. Feel warmth spread in your chest, a glow of connectedness. This is your Song singing praise for growth, for the gift of "not knowing and ready to find."

EMBRACE THE BEAUTY

Feel the beauty of this openness—the joy of discovery, the calm excitement of wonder. It's the Field shimmering through you, the universe's banquet vast and inviting. Let it shake the lies loose from you and deepen your awareness all at once.

FIND THE TRUTH
UNDERNEATH THE DISGUISE

Feeling gratitude through your belly and heart, let your art tell the story, showing your challenge between the arrogance mask and your Song nature. What did that feel like? Is your perspective different now?

CHAPTER 10
CULTIVATING POSITIVE PERCEPTION

Looking Through The Lens Of Lack

Negative perceptions paint the world as broken, hostile, a place of "less-than." They're a cocktail of the other "No Nos," frosted with victimhood. Yet, as we awaken, we see the lie: the world is alive with beauty and love, and we're powerful creators, not powerless victims.

Shifting perception unveils the mind-blowing beauty and power of the world—a tsunami of splendor, the passion and delight of existence woven into every atom.

Why It Matters

This ugly mindset traps us in a dark hole, blind to our Song and humanity's potential. Stepping outside it, we build a new world from truth and daring invention. As Jeff Booth, author of *The Price of Tomorrow* says, "Broken information can't fix a broken system." And the ancients said, "Negative perceptions can't fix or inform anything." We must see anew, transforming our hearts and lives and minds—*weaving and feeling* the power of beauty into the Field, the Web of Life.

The Garden Shift

My little yard was a disaster—tangled weeds choking the flowers, toys strewn like confetti and a tomato plant drooping in defeat. I'd stare at it from the porch, a knot of disappointment tightening in my gut.

"A good renter would fix this," I thought, judging myself against an ideal I couldn't meet. The mess felt like a personal failing, a mirror of my scattered life.

One afternoon, tired of the guilt, I tried something Chea said—a different lens.

I sat down, closed my eyes, and let the "shoulds" fall away. When I looked again, I didn't see failure—I saw life. Ants marched in busy lines, wildflowers poked defiantly through the chaos, a breeze rustled the leaves in a dance of resilience.

The yard wasn't broken; it was thriving, raw and unscripted. My frustration melted into awe, then peace. I wasn't separate from this wildness; I was part of it.

That shift—from seeing the world as a dark, worthless, ruined cage to a place full of magic and aliveness—freed me to hear my Song among the garden's untamed chorus, singing together. I felt the beauty of what is—the thrill of life moving forward, the peace of letting go of the programming—because I could see, *I could feel*, our pure existence had always been sacred.

PRACTICE 8

SEEING BEAUTY EVEN IN THE DARK CLOUDS OF A STORM

You are sacred.

This space you make for these spiritual tasks is sacred.

These tasks of finding yourself, of learning to feel your Song, are sacred.

Get relaxed and nicely comfortable, breathe slowly and deeply. Keep re-focusing your attention back on your task and its goal of waking up out of your negative perceptions. Keep intending to remember your experiences. Don't overthink it. Feel it. And keep feeling it.

NOTICE NEGATIVITY

Spot a dark thought—like "Nothing works out" or "This is awful." Pause and hold it lightly, no blame. Where does it hit you—a lump in your throat, a slump in your shoulders?

Negative perceptions are a trap. An addiction. An expression of powerlessness. An illusion. This is the shadow creeping in—the mind thief—the beast.

FEEL IT

Lean into the feeling behind the thought—fear, tiredness, old habit? Let it swell up, then fade with a slow breath. Don't fight it; let it pass like a dissipating cloud. This is your Song sweeping the slate clean.

REFRAME

Hunt for one spark of beauty here—maybe "Someone's trying" or "The sun's still shining." It can be tiny, a whisper of light. Feel it take root—does your chest lift, your eyes soften? This is the shift beginning.

AMPLIFY

Focus on that beauty and let it grow. Picture it as a warm glow spreading from your heart, filling you up. Feel the change—breathe deeper, notice your mind clearing as negativity shrinks in the light of beauty.

Remembering the luring feeling of your own Song calling you, taking all the power away from the beliefs—*returning it to you.*

EMBRACE THE BEAUTY

Soak in the beauty of this moment—the strength that comes from hope, the soothingness of seeing anew. It's the gifts of beauty unfolding, turning ashes into gold. Let it wrap around you like a warm embrace.

UNCOVER THE PRECIOUSNESS YOU HID

Find it again. Free it. Bring it into the light. Show this adventure, let your art tell your story. Express this moment in your life, and mostly, *feel it.*

PART THREE

DEEPENING THE PRACTICE OF THE 7 NO NOS

CHAPTER 11

SONG AND
THE SPIRIT SENSES

Your Sacred Totality

Lonnie first felt her Song on a crisp morning in the forest, leaning against an old pine, its bark smooth against her back. The world was still, save for the rustle of leaves and the scent of damp earth. She closed her eyes and let her thoughts quiet, reaching into her feelings—and there it was....

A whispering thunder, not heard but felt, deep in her core. It was warm, timeless—her "sacred Totality," the "mysteries of her Being" beyond all masks—*it was the feeling of her own Song....*

She recognized it.

She even felt like she was remembering it.

The pre-flood Egyptian teachings speak of 360 spirit senses—subtle ways to perceive beyond the physical. As she sat, she felt the tree's Song, steady and grounded, and the wind's Song, dancing yet alive. The forest wasn't silent; it sang without sound, and she was woven into its melody.

This wasn't a concept to grasp—it was an experience, a remembering of her connectedness to all things. Feeling her Song, she realized, was the path to awakening these senses, a birthright calling her home.

When you are deep in the feeling of your Song, your spirit senses begin their awakening to the beauty of what real aliveness is—your palpable connectedness that stirs your love with passion—the lingering, luring dance of the Songs of all creation. Just *feeling* this beauty as it stretches out into the Web ignites your consciousness.

PRACTICE 9
FEELING YOUR SONG

Let's find out more about the feeling of your unique Song. Get settled into your sacred space. Relax. Keep re-focusing your attention back on your task and its goal of waking up out of the fog of blind beliefs. Intend to stay awake. And intend to remember your experiences and their feelings. Don't get trapped in analytical thinking and words. Keep it sacred—the key is in the feeling—so feel everything deeply.

Keep feeling!—Keep feeling!—Keep feeling!

FINDING THE FEELING OF YOUR SONG

Find a peaceful spot—maybe by a window, under a tree, or in a cozy corner. Quiet your mind. Close your eyes and let your breath slow down, like waves lapping at the shore. Let your thoughts drift away, one by one, and *feel* into what has made you be happy, or feel full of love, or passion, or excitement—even the "falling in love feeling."

Let this beautiful feeling grow and fill your being. *Feeling and knowing the truth of that special feeling is the key.* That is actually the feeling of you—the feeling of your Song—it's not what is outside you, nor is it the other person who you are only partially having your attention on.

That beautiful, authentic feeling is the feeling of you. This is the sacred space inside you where you can explore your Song and all of creation. This is the truth of who you are.

FEEL

Hold the feeling. Keep your attention inward. What's alive in you right now? Something you can't put a name to that permeates deeper than words can reach? Don't label it—don't stop— just *feel* it. This is your Song, your private, individual, unique piece of Creator.

EXPAND

Hold the feeling. Now, don't let go of your Song. Let your Song reach out. Feel the energy of something *non-human* near you—a plant, a tree, a stone—and hold your Song. You are following your connectedness. What does it feel like? Does it feel like anything you can put a word to? Let your intuition guide you. You are feeling the Songs around you conversing with your Song.

CONNECT

Imagine a light connecting your Song to this other energy. Feel the exchange—does it spark joy, calm, curiosity? You and the other are exchanging energies. This is the Web of Life, the dance of Songs, touching, weaving together, deepening your sense of belonging.

EMBRACE THE BEAUTY

Hold the feeling. Notice the beauty in the connectedness—the wonder of all this friendship, the excitement and belonging, of being part of something vast. It's the universe's banquet, rich with flavors of life, and discoveries that surprise, enrich and lovingly haunt you with the awe of it all. Let it fill you with a taste of the sacred. Gift them your gratefulness.

TAKE IT MUCH DEEPER

What did you feel? Speak it with your creations. What surprised you? Is your world any different now? Make as many pieces of art as you need, keep pouring it out until it feels finished.

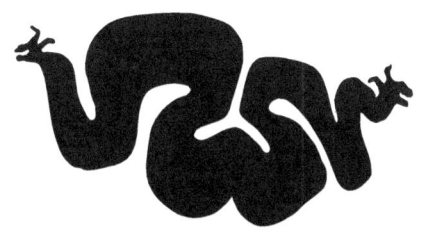

CHAPTER 12

ANCIENT MONEY – ANCIENT BELIEFS

The Corruption That Creeped In While Most Never Noticed

Money had always been a mystery to my friend Donna, a lesson from childhood that it was scarce and slippery. She didn't know what to do with it. She was afraid of losing it, and she tied her worth to the amounts she had. Those ideas and beliefs drove years of questionable choices—like feeling guilty over little splurges.

Then came a crossroads: she could spend some of her money on a writing course she longed for or save it "for safety." Her old fear said no, but she paused, feeling into her Song. What did she truly want? What could she use now *and* into the future that she would cherish the most, use the most? She wanted to seek growth, not stagnation.

So she chose the course, her hands shaking as she paid. It was a risk, but it felt in sync to her. The experience cracked open new paths—skills, connections, a joy she had never known—and the money returned tenfold in unexpected ways.

More than that, it shifted her lens on wealth. When she moved from the fear fog to clarity, money became a current, not a cage. Aligning with her truth revealed the beauty of abundance everywhere—the variety and flavors of life's banquet, a cosmic force flowing through the Field of Life, available to you at any time.

This wasn't a concept to grasp—it was an experience.

PRACTICE 10
ALIGNING WITH TRUTH

It's time for the bigger shoes now. Get comfy. Breathe slowly and evenly. Let your mind empty of the daily rush. As soon as you realize your attention has drifted, re-focus back on your task and its goal of waking up out of the blind beliefs. Be truly honest with yourself and your memories—don't judge yourself or others. Intend to remember your experiences. Quiet your mind and its words. Keep it sacred—this is the time to feel for the truth of things.

EXAMINE MONEY BELIEFS

Sit with a piece of paper and list your beliefs about money—like "It's hard to get," or "I don't deserve it" or "Money's evil." Let them come without judgment, like leaves floating downstream. Notice how each one feels—does it tighten your chest, quicken your breath? This is the old story, the old lies speaking.

QUESTION THEM

For each belief, ask "Is this mine, or did I inherit it?" Think back—whose voice is this, a parent's worry, a teacher's lesson? Then ask "Does this serve me now?" Feel the energy—does it lift or drag? Your Song is nudging you toward truth.

FEEL THE ABUNDANCE OF LOVE AND BEAUTY EVERYWHERE

Step outside or look out a window. See the abundance in nature—leaves dancing and reflecting the sunlight, stars shining boundless energy, grains of sand holding the records of time, everything flowing, mixing, sharing. Let it sink in—the beauty and abundance within the universe is mind-blowing. While holding deep gratitude, feel that same abundance and beauty in you—your breath, your heartbeat, your endless potential—it's all your Song's gift.

ACT

Make one small choice that reflects this abundance—a step toward a dream, perhaps. Feel the shift—does your heart open, your step lighten? This is your Song aligning with the flow of the universe.

EMBRACE THE BEAUTY

Notice the beauty in this act—the adventure of growth, the peace of not worrying, rich with possibilities. Let yourself feel your genuine gratitude, it is a taste of true wealth, the riches of your Song.

FIND THE DEPTHS OF YOUR NEW EXPERIENCES

Let your Song talk to you through your art. Let it be rich and full of passion. What did it feel like to choose? Show what it was like to feel such abundance and beauty. What beauty did you find in abundance? Let your Song celebrate, expressing itself, capturing this moment.

CHAPTER 13
LIVING IN HARMONY

Dreaming the Dream—A New World

Picture a morning where the 7 No Nos are alive in every breath. You wake to sunlight streaming through your window, the air buzzing with a quiet harmony. Outside, your neighbor greets you—not with polite distance, but with a warmth that needs no words. There's no judgment in their gaze, no rush to compare. You walk to a shared garden, where hands dig into soil not for gain but for love of the act. Voices weave stories, free of assumptions, rich with discernment and flowing with gratitude.

In this world, their wealth flows to nurture dreams, not to hoard or flaunt. People see each other's

Songs—unique and sacred—and honor them without envy. The Earth thrives alongside us, its rivers clean, its creatures creating balance. This isn't a fantasy; it's a seed of gratitude we plant with every choice.

I feel it in my bones—a vision of an ever-balancing dance toward unity, possible if we live these No Nos now. It begins with us, today, awakening to a world we can create together. A harmonious world is a tapestry of beauty—a contagious dance of connectedness and fireworks of awakening Songs, a tsunami of love and creativity, nurturing our planet for eons.

PRACTICE 11
SONG TO SONG – HEART TO HEART

This is all about unconditional love and unconditional acceptance. Feel all the love around you. Keep re-focusing back on your task and its goal of waking up. Be truly honest with yourself and your memories—don't judge yourself or others. We are always connected to everybody and everything, but today we are going to make this connection *conscious and purposeful—sending and receiving—giving and accepting.* Intend to remember your experiences and their feelings. Don't get trapped in analytical thinking and words. *Keep it sacred—feel everything—give love—feel love!*

CONNECT

Today, feel another's Song—maybe a friend, a stranger, even a pet. Close your eyes for a moment and sense their energy. What's unique about it—gentle, steady, vibrant? Let your heart reach out, like a hand touching another's hand. You are feeling the dance of Songs touching.

SHARE LOVE

Send a silent blessing their way—a warm light, a kind thought, a wish for their joy. Feel it flow from your heart to theirs, no strings attached. Notice how it shifts you—does your chest soften, your breath deepen? This is you, your Song, weaving love into the Web of Life.

DREAM

Imagine a world where everyone lives this way—awake, connected, loving. Picture the streets, the homes, the laughter. Feel the harmony, the beauty of it—like the universe's banquet in full bloom. Let it inspire you, a glimpse of what's possible—a glimpse into the future we are building, we're dreaming the dream that forms the future.

COMMIT

Renew your vow to your path of growth. Say it softly: "I choose to live the No Nos, to awaken my Song, to weave a better world." Feel the words settle in your bones, a promise to yourself and the universe. This is your Song's pledge.

EMBRACE THE BEAUTY

Notice the wonders in this vision—the passion in beauty, the heart stirrings and depths of harmony, the inherent love throughout the universe. It's the Web of Life glowing, the universe's banquet laid out for all. Let it fill you with hope, a feast of the sacred.

DREAM THE DREAM

Dream the dream. Create with the endless palette of your imagination. What does this new world look like to you? How does it feel? What role do you play? What are the Songs of others like? Explore Song to Song—one to one—with the trees, the flowers and herbs, your pets and animals in the wild. Feel the Song of each one. Feel their Songs as they mingle with your own Song. Feel the gratitude. How does this inform you about the future? About your dream?

A LAST MELODY

THE SYMPHONY OF YOUR AWAKENING

You've journeyed through these pages, stepping into the garden of your Song, feeling the steady pulse of your attention, and diving into the boundless ocean of unconditional love.

The 7 No Nos have been your companions—gentle guides whispering invitations to shed the masks, question the shadows, and embrace the truth of who you are. This isn't the end of the path; it's the beginning of a symphony, one where your unique melody weaves into the vast harmony of all existence.

Each "No No" has been a note in this awakening—a call to peel away blind beliefs and judgments, to release expectations and assumptions, to pause before conclusions, to let go of arrogance, and to see beauty where shadows once loomed.

Together, they've tuned your awareness, aligning it with the ancient rhythm of your Song: that sacred, vibrant essence that connects you to the Web of Life, to Neith's tapestry of love, to the banquet of the universe laid out before us all.

You've felt it, haven't you? That stirring deep within, that haunting beauty that hums through your bones, reminding you of your place in the dance of creation.

This journey is yours to live, not just to read. The 7 No Nos are not rigid laws but living melodies—tools to carry into your days, your relationships and your dreams. When the world pulls you toward chaos, when old habits creep in, return to these tools. Question with courage, feel with openness and love without conditions.

Let your attention be your power, your Song your compass, and beauty your guide. Every step you take ripples outward, touching the Songs around you, weaving a new world thread by thread.

Imagine this: a life where you wake each morning attuned to your essence, where your choices reflect the clarity of your truth, where love flows from you like a river unbound. Picture a community—a humanity—awakened alongside you, each Song shining, each voice adding to the chorus.

This isn't a distant dream; it's a possibility born from the small, brave acts of awakening you choose today. You are not alone in this. The Hetakas, the ancient Egyptians, the countless keepers of wisdom across time—they walk with you, their voices echoing in these teachings, cheering you on.

The beauty of this path is that it's yours to shape. Your Song is ancient, vast, and ever growing, a spark of the Creator's love that no mask can dim.

As you live the 7 No Nos, you'll uncover more of its notes—new depths of passion, peace, and connectedness. You'll feel the tsunami of love that floods the cosmos, the same love and splendor that lives in you. This is your birthright: to awaken, to transform, and to share your melody with a world hungry for harmony.

So, take a breath. Feel your Song right now—its warmth, its rhythm, its quiet power. Step forward with it, not as a solitary traveler, but as a weaver in the great tapestry of life. The 7 No Nos are your threads, love your needle, beauty your vision.

Together, we're not just remembering who we are—we're singing a new era into being, one breathtaking note at a time.

The banquet is set, the music is playing, and your place at the table is waiting.

Welcome home.

PETROGLYPH INDEX
ILLUSTRATED BY KAY CORDELL WHITAKER

© All illustrations are the exclusive rights of Kay Cordell Whitaker. Usage of these illustrations or their likeness is not allowed without written consent from Kay Cordell Whitaker.

SPIRIT BOAT
P. 5, 58, 112, 153

KOKOPELLIS
P. 1, 59, 115, 151

DOOR MAKER
P. 9, 25, 97

DRUMMING
KOKOPELLI.
P. 20, 137

JOURNEY MAN
P. 11, 60, 123

SONG BIRD
P. 21, 90

BIRTHING
P. 23, 100

MOON SPIRIT
P. 22, 107, 133

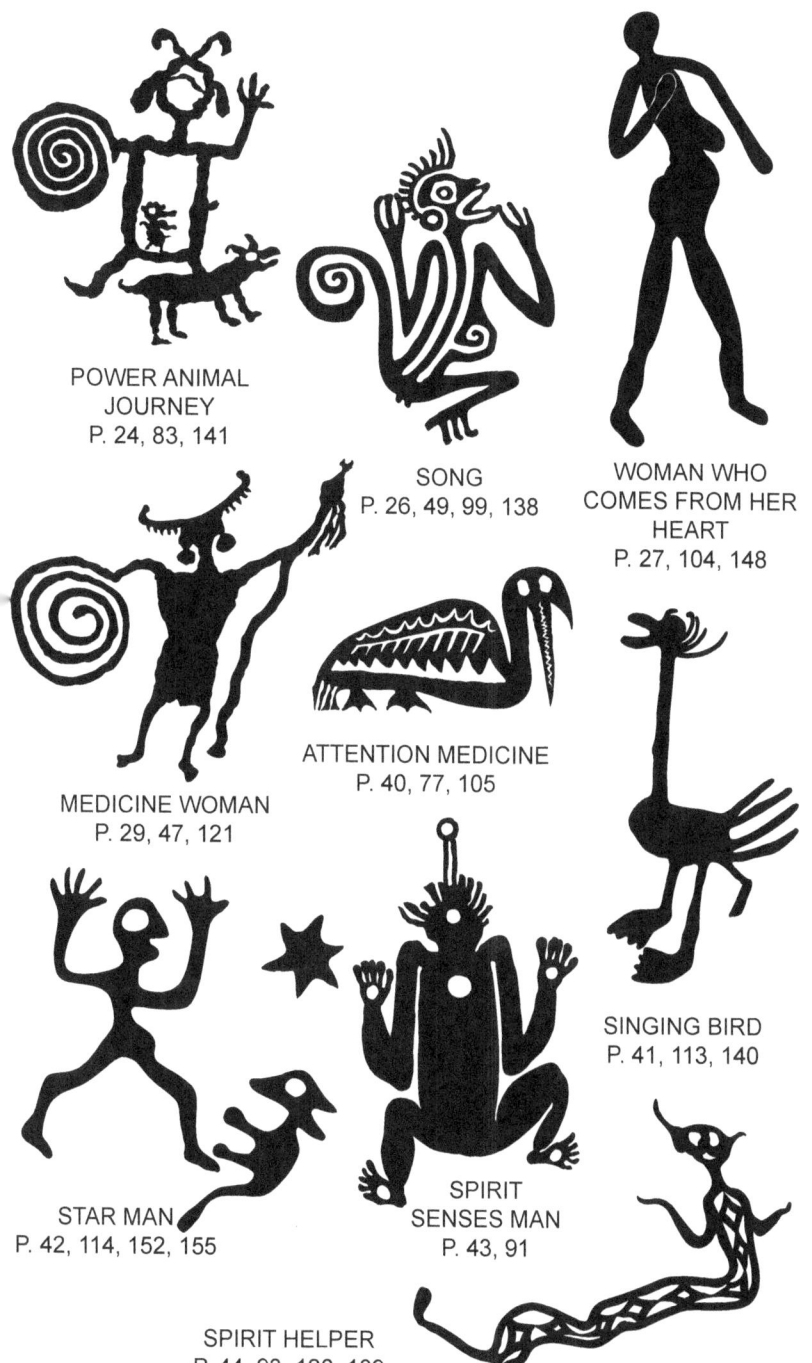

POWER ANIMAL
JOURNEY
P. 24, 83, 141

SONG
P. 26, 49, 99, 138

WOMAN WHO
COMES FROM HER
HEART
P. 27, 104, 148

MEDICINE WOMAN
P. 29, 47, 121

ATTENTION MEDICINE
P. 40, 77, 105

SINGING BIRD
P. 41, 113, 140

STAR MAN
P. 42, 114, 152, 155

SPIRIT
SENSES MAN
P. 43, 91

SPIRIT HELPER
P. 44, 93, 120, 139

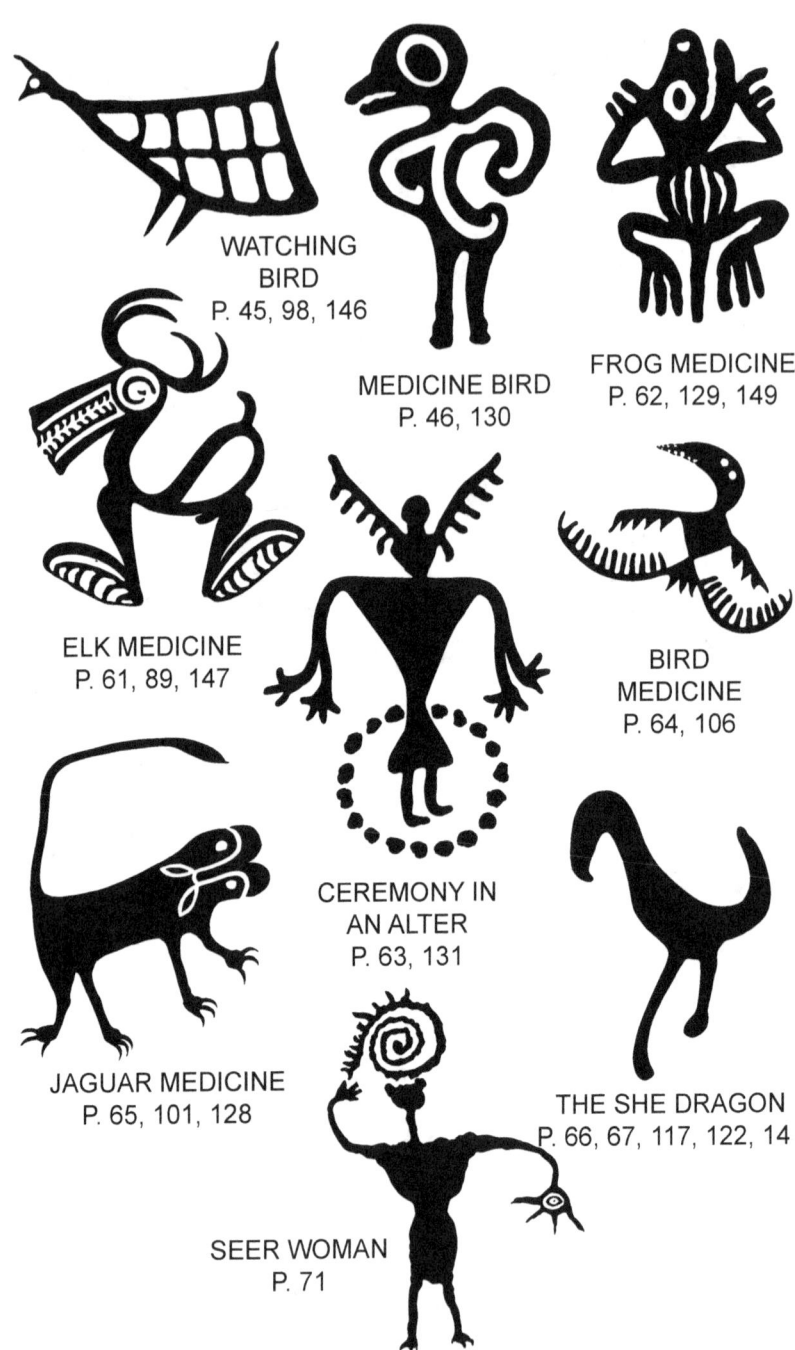

WATCHING
BIRD
P. 45, 98, 146

MEDICINE BIRD
P. 46, 130

FROG MEDICINE
P. 62, 129, 149

ELK MEDICINE
P. 61, 89, 147

BIRD
MEDICINE
P. 64, 106

CEREMONY IN
AN ALTER
P. 63, 131

JAGUAR MEDICINE
P. 65, 101, 128

THE SHE DRAGON
P. 66, 67, 117, 122, 14

SEER WOMAN
P. 71

SPIRIT HELPER
WITH MEDICINE
P. 73, 87

WATER
PLANET MAN
P. 78

EARTH
FIRE SERPENT
P. 82, 143, 154

TWO
HEADED BIRD
P. 79

SONG CAT
P. 68, 88, 125

HAND
MEDICINE
P. 80

TEACHER
WOMAN
P. 81, 109

Kay Cordell Whitaker is an elder, grandmother, and the only known lineage keeper of Ka Ta See in the modern world, an ancient spiritual tradition with roots in Peru, Lemuria, and the Egyptian Mystery Teachings. For more than five decades, she has lived, practiced, and taught wisdom that was safeguarded for thousands of years and entrusted to her by her adoptive grandparents and teachers, Domano and Chea Hetaka of Peru, as well as a Berber wisdom keeper from Egypt.

As head of The School of Ka Ta See and its lead instructor, Whitaker has dedicated her life to helping people release destructive patterns, reclaim their sovereignty, and reconnect with their Song—the vibrant essence of who they are. Her teaching style is warm, nonjudgmental, and experiential, making ancient practices accessible to seekers of all backgrounds. Whether in live workshops, online classes, or through her writing, Whitaker's mission is clear: to share the practices of Ka Ta See and the teachings of Isis so that individuals can remember their truth and weave lives of love, beauty, and freedom.

Whitaker is the author of three acclaimed books—*The Reluctant Shaman, Sacred Link,* and *The Weavings: Dawn of a New World*—each offering a deeper look into the ancient knowledge she carries. Teaching since 1987, Whitaker has guided thousands of students from across the globe—including Europe, Asia, and Australia—through ceremonies, healing practices, and the rediscovery of their own innate wisdom. Today, she continues to write, teach, and inspire through her company, A World In Balance, while also enjoying her role as a great-grandmother.

To learn more about Whitaker's teachings, visit www.katasee. com and connect with her growing community online.

WANT TO LEARN MORE ABOUT YOUR SONG?

JOIN THE COMMUNITY!

GO TO WWW.THE7NONOS.COM TO:

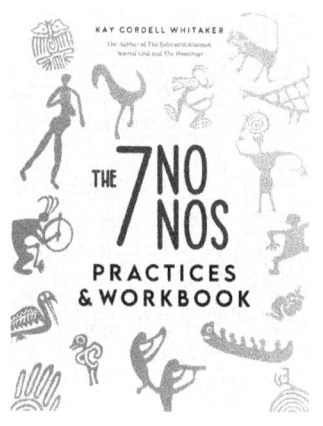

Register to
**RECEIVE A FREE
THE 7 NO NOS
DOWNLOADABLE
PRACTICES &
WORKBOOK**

Register to **JOIN OUR FREE ONLINE COMMUNITY** to:

CONNECT with others practicing and sharing about their experiences,

Participate in upcoming **SONG CEREMONIES** and other events led by Kay Cordell Whitaker,

Receive a **FREE 7 NO NOS POSTER**,

And so much more!

Thank you for reading

THE 7 NO NOS
A GUIDE TO AWAKENING AND FREEDOM

We hope this book inspired you and that you will continue to read it over and over again, finding new insights and understanding each time.

If you enjoyed *The 7 No Nos—A Guide To Awakening And Freedom*, we would sincerely appreciate it if you took the time to review it on Goodreads or the retail site you purchased this book on and help these teachings reach more people like you.

To review on social media use **#The7NoNos and @katasee.**

Want to learn more about these ancient teachings?

SUBSCRIBE TO OUR CHANNEL

Join us for our regular
Healing Talks at
youtube.com/@kaycordellwhitaker

THE SCHOOL OF KA TA SEE

LEARN FORGOTTEN MYSTERIES
DEVELOP SPIRITUAL SOVEREIGNTY
HEAL THE WORLD

Whether you are seeking a deeper understanding, health, peace, and beauty that comes with learning more about your true identity, or have the desire to step into the Ancient Healing Arts of Ka Ta See and the predynastic Egyptian Teachings, or you want to help effect the healing of our planet, the teachings and practices through the School of Ka Ta See courses and ceremonies offer those opportunities.

You can learn more about
The School of Ka Ta See at
www.katasee.world/KaTaSeeEnrollment

To learn more about Ka Ta See and other opportunities to work with and learn from Kay, visit
www.katasee.com
or www.linktr.ee/katasee

MORE OPPORTUNITIES TO READ AND LEARN

THE RELUCTANT SHAMAN—A WOMAN'S FIRST ENCOUNTERS WITH THE UNSEEN SPIRITS OF THE EARTH

This is Kay Cordell Whitaker's spellbinding account of her "reluctant" apprenticeship to Domano and Chea Hetaka, two charismatic shamans from the Western Amazon who come to teach her—a young homemaker—to be a Kala Keh Nah Seh, a "Weaver of Webs of Balance," and to hand down the ancient wisdom of their people. In spite of her doubts and fears, Whitaker finds the balance and harmony she was destined to know.

SACRED LINK—JOINING FORTUNES WITH THE UNKNOWN

In this rich and compelling second book, Kay Cordell Whitaker continues the spiritual journey that enthralled readers of *The Reluctant Shaman*. The Hetakas, the humorously wise couple who led Whitaker to her awakening are back, drawing their willing pupil still further into their irresistible yet often terrifying dance. As Whitaker learns to embrace her gifts, she is able to see how our dominant cultures have kept humanity captive in a soul-numbing prison, unaware of the power and extraordinary opportunity that awaits it. With the help (and prodding) of her demanding but sage mentors, Whitaker uncovers the secret to igniting our physical senses—a discovery so potent it will allow all of humanity to join the Hetakas' ride into the *Forbidden Paradise*.

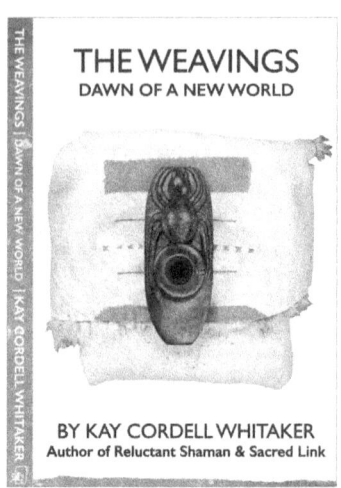

THE WEAVINGS — DAWN OF A NEW WORLD

This book is a guiding light for personal and collective transformation. It offers a riveting body of teachings from the spirits about creating a life and a world based on self-sovereignty, love and profound personal healing. It urges us to unite as a community to achieve a common goal, laying the foundation and creating the blueprint for a new humanity and our new world.

Both the ancient teachings of Ka Ta See and the pre-flood Egyptian Mystery Teachings clearly state that we are living through the end of our current world, the current era, and the beginning of a new world, as do many teachings from ancient traditional cultures around the globe. This is not a distant prophecy but a reality unfolding before us.

All these ancient teachings refer to this time as the bridge time, the time between worlds, and we, the people living today, aware of its significance, are the bridge builders to that new world.

AWAKEN TO LOVE, BEAUTY, AND CONNECTION THROUGH ANCIENT WISDOM.

Long before modern culture drowned us in fear and judgment, the ancients carried a different map for being human. Hidden within traditions from ancient civilizations is a quiet, powerful antidote to the disconnection so many feel today. Once secret, these teachings are now being shared with you—right on time.

The 7 No Nos offers a practical and joyful way to break free. Rooted in shamanism and the Egyptian Mystery Teachings, these seven timeless principles show you how to let go of the patterns that block love and peace. Presented with humor, stories, and creative practices, they help you reconnect with your true essence—your Song.

Kay Cordell Whitaker, the only lineage holder of Ka Ta See in the modern world, brings forward the ancient wisdom to guide you in discovering freedom, beauty, and self-sovereignty.

LEARN TO:

> Drop blind beliefs that weigh you down.

> Release judgments and open your heart.

> Step out of expectations and assumptions.

> Stop conclusions that distort your truth.

> See beauty where negativity once ruled.

THIS BOOK IS FOR SEEKERS, WORLD CHANGERS, AND THE SPIRITUALLY CURIOUS WHO ARE READY TO AWAKEN TO LOVE, CLARITY, AND JOY.

KAY CORDELL WHITAKER is an elder, grandmother, and the only known lineage keeper of the ancient Ka Ta See tradition in the modern world. For over 40 years, she has taught students worldwide how to release fear, reconnect with love, and live from their Song—the truth of who they are. She is the author of *The Reluctant Shaman*, *Sacred Link*, and *The Weavings*.

LEARN MORE AT
KATASEE.COM

ISBN 978-1-970928-00-6   US$16.99

5 1 6 9 9 >

9 781970 928006